KETTY LESTER

From Arkansas to
Grammy-nominated "Love Letters" to
Little House on the Prairie

A Memoir

Ketty Lester

Copyright ©2020 by Revoyda F. Buckley
Los Angeles, California
All rights reserved
Printed and Bound in the United States of America

Published and Distributed by:
Elite Publishing House
Los Angeles, California
Email: KettyLester11@yahoo.com

Packaging/Consulting:
Professional Publishing House
1425 W. Manchester Ave. Ste. B
Los Angeles, California 90047
323-750-3592
Email: professionalpublishinghouse@yahoo.com
www.professionalpublishinghouse.com

Cover & Interior Design: Jessica Tilles/TWASolutions.com
First printing September 2020
Second printing September 2022
978-0-578-66233-6
10 9 8 7 6 5 4 3 2 1

No part of this book may be reproduced, stored in a retrieval system or transmitted in any form or by any means without the prior written permission of the publisher—except by a reviewer who may quote brief passages in a review to be printed in a newspaper, magazine or journal.

For inquiries contact: KettyLester11@yahoo.com

Acknowledgments

I want to thank God because He is the Lord our God, He made us and He knows all about us. I thank Him for giving me the strength, the determination, desire, and the goodwill to not give up on writing my life story. Maybe it will not be all that I wanted but it is what God gave me to do, to say and it is the truth. I have been blessed with my friends who have encouraged me to tell my story. And that gave me the desire and, with God's help, the will to do it. I hope you will enjoy it. God bless you.

Then to Dr. Marin Luther King, Jr., who fought so hard for voting rights. He accomplished that goal and then started fighting the movie industry about the average Black woman. Before he started this fight, if you were not light-skinned or fat, you had very little chance in show business, except for singing in night clubs and then one would have to sing in a certain place. But with the help of Dr. King, I had a chance to walk through the door of commercials. Thanks to his doing and my record "Love Letter" at that time. God bless Dr. King for the help he gave me.

To Nancy Leotta; she was just one of my fans, and now I consider her a friend. She wrote me a letter and then she came to see me. She put me on Facebook and she continues to find ways to help me in so many ways. She has found out that it is not easy to get an old Black artist's book published—she tried and I thank her and I am so grateful for her help. She is not a quitter and she's not asking for money. In fact, she paid for what she tried to do for me herself. Bless you, Nancy, and I appreciate what you are trying to do to help me.

To Dr. Rosie Milligan; when I thought the possibility of getting my book published had come to an end and it was all over, my church gave me a name and telephone number of someone I didn't know existed—Dr. Rosie Milligan. Dr. Milligan has helped so many to birth their Book Baby. She has been a true blessing to me and I consider her a true friend. I feel blessed to have her in my life. She is the one that made my book publishing possible. I pray for Dr. Rosie; she has so much to do for others. I almost feel that I am in her way, but God will bring us through it all.

To Jessica Tilles, thank you for all that you have done such as editing my book, doing the research, and bringing this book to its completion. God bless you and I am so grateful for all your help. I had a picture of Dorothy Shay but I lost it, but you found a picture of her doing your research. I had not heard from Dorothy Shay since I played at that Village Vanguard, but looking at this picture you found, I know that she lived longer than I thought she did. My reason for saying this is because when I met Dorothy in the 1960s, they were wearing slim heels and pointed-toe shoes not like what

Acknowledgments

she was wearing in the picture. Thanks to your research, though, and unfortunately, I learned that Dorothy Shay died in 1978.

To my friend, Josephine Drake, I can never say enough about you because you have been there with me from the beginning until this day. You have always been there for me in every way—and I thank you. One cannot have a better friend than what you have been to me. You are my dearest friend and may God continue to bless you.

TABLE OF CONTENTS

Introduction 11

PART ONE

The Beginning of My Life: Happy Days 21
The Farm and The Depression 21
The War 33
High School and Hope 39
Thinking About the Past, and Looking
    Toward the Future 47

PART TWO

Starting College and Turning Pro 56
From Revoyda to Ketty 56
From Co-Ed to Club Girl 63
Los Angeles, Stars, and Very Fine Gowns 70

PART THREE

First Recording and First Boyfriend 76
Someone to Write Love Letters to 88

PART FOUR

My Two Big Mistakes and Marriage,
    Motherhood, Movies, and TV 110
Family Values 110
One Last Love Letter and A Brand-New Love 118

Two New Arrivals—A Baby Boy and Epilepsy 124
The Magic of Black Television and Movies 136
The Juggling Years—My Family, and Extended
    Ones, Too 144
More Film Work, Loss, and *Little House On*
    the Prairie 154

PART FIVE

The End of Time 173
Farewell, Bill 182

PART SIX

Yesterday, Today, and Tomorrow 189
Nobody Told Me the Music Business Changed 189
Doing Unto Others, Like The Bible Says 196
Looking After My Family, Looking After Myself 199

PART SEVEN

All My Love, Ketty 205

Pictorial 211

Filmography 225

Introduction

Who is Ketty Lester?

Well, she is a former singer, and television and screen actress, who was the first Black woman to perform on television as a singer on Grouch Marx's show, *You Bet Your Life* in 1957, and to appear in national commercials. She started her show business career in the late fifties at the University of California, Berkeley, then went on to share the stage at The Purple Onion in San Francisco with Maya Angelou and Phyllis Diller. In 1957, she became the first Black woman to have a featured spot in The Ziegfeld Follies since Josephine Baker, and the first Black woman to 'break type' in national television commercials, putting to rest the 'mammy' stereotype, and the myth that lighter skinned Black women are more attractive and acceptable. Her 1961 hit single, "Love Letters" made her an international star, topping the charts in both the USA and the UK, and is still widely played today. She guest starred on many ground-breaking television shows, such as *Julia* and *Sanford and Son*, became a regular on the long running soap opera, *Days of Our Lives*, and starred as Hester-Sue on *Little House On The Prairie*.

Ketty was the first celebrity to speak out, and educate the public about epilepsy, a condition she has been living with for many years.

Where is Ketty Lester now?

Right here. Writing to you. Now retired, I am a believer in God, and I love to watch television. I don't mix well with people, maybe one person at a time. Maybe you would consider me a loner. If I don't say I will or can do something, don't expect it. If I say I will do something, I try to live up to what I say. If you say you like me, but I can't depend on you, that is a lie. The Bible says, "Thou shalt not lie."

My mother and father raised me according to the Ten Commandments, which I still try to live by, but people are different now. They live in a way I don't quite understand. God said there would be a change in men and women. So, be it.

Why did I decide to write my own memoir?

Well, this is a simple book about me, my family, my career, and the life I have had and enjoyed. There's been a lot of sadness, mistakes, loneliness, and hurt, but without that, there would be no book, would there? Without all that, there would be no "Love Letters," so this book is my Love Letter to you.

It's important to me because it gives the true details of my life from my childhood in the country to now. There is so much on Facebook and the Internet about me that I did not put out, and

Introduction

don't know who did. Some of it true, some of it not. I hope this Love Letter teaches you a few things; what it was like to grow up Black in the depression, what it was like to be a woman alone, a Black woman, trying to make her way in the big city, and get into show business in the 1950s and 1960s. I hope that my life teaches you that it doesn't matter who you are, or where you come from, that if you believe in yourself, and in God, you can overcome any obstacle, and weather any storm.

What am I most remembered for?

God has blessed me to have done a lot in my lifetime, but I'm most remembered for my 1961 recording of "Love Letters Straight From Your Heart," which stayed on the charts in the United States and the United Kingdom for about three years, and people still remember it today. The next most-remembered performance was the first horror movie for Blacks in 1972, *Blacula*. I had a lead role, playing Juanita Jones, a vampire, in that movie. The third role, which was my last, was as Hester-Sue Terhune on the long-running television series, *The Little House on the Prairie*, from 1977 to 1983. I played the only Black female teacher in the series.

I still get a little residual income from that show—not much, but I get some. What do I *want* to be remembered for? I'd like to be remembered as a 'door opener;' as someone who paved the way for other Black American women, women of color, and any woman facing obstacles in their lives. I'd like to be remembered for living my life as a good woman, and not compromising myself to get what I got.

Does Ketty Lester have an Internet presence?
Oh, yes! I'm on the Internet:
   www.facebook.com/misskettylester
  official website: www.misskettylester.com.

My Family Tree

I don't know how many years after my maternal grandmother, Callie, died when my grandfather, Namon, remarried a woman named Mattie (last name unknown to me). They had children—my half-aunts and uncles. The first one's name was John Montgomery, then CL Montgomery, then Osceola Montgomery, then Aleane Montgomery, then Perry Montgomery, and their last child was Olamay Montgomery.

I met all of them during my lifetime—the full aunts and uncles and the half- uncles and aunts. The one I knew best was Uncle CL, but I didn't know what CL stood for. I just knew him as Uncle CL. He started a church for family and friends. I don't know the denomination. He was the preacher and also a contractor.

I also met my step-grandmother on my mother's side. That was Mattie. I met all my half-uncles and aunts later in life. I have

Introduction

included pictures of the full aunts and uncles in this book. They all lived in different places when I was born. Raised with my father's family—Grandfather Gram and Grandmother Amanda—we always went to our church, the St. Paul AME Church

Introduction

Amanda and Gram Frierson.

Ketty Lester

Mamon Montgomery

Introduction

PART ONE

The Beginning of My Life: Happy Days

The Farm and The Depression

I believe I was born to live and have a minimum amount of success. I have never been brilliant, smart, or considered beautiful. I have had some bad luck, but I am trying to change the bad luck to good. Now, why am I trying to write this book? I don't know, but I know that this is hard. My memories of childhood in Arkansas, are as clear as if it was yesterday, even though it was such a long time ago.

I was born on a farm in Arkansas between Patmos and Hope in 1934. I don't know for sure, but I learned that my paternal grandfather, Gram Frierson, owned six hundred acres of land back in his day. He was a minister and was married to a lady named Amanda Smith. She was a half-breed—half Black-American and half Indian. They had three sons and one daughter. Gram lost three hundred acres of his land to save his three sons. They went to jail because someone said they whistled at a White woman. My father and his two brothers did not do that. They knew better, but the White people wanted land and that's the way they got it; one hundred acres per child to get them out of prison. At his death, Gram had given his sons eighty acres each of the land and sixty acres to his one daughter.

My father, Arthur Frierson, was the oldest of the three boys. My mother was Pearl Montgomery. Her father, Namon Montgomery, was an ex-slave, who was also a half-breed—the son of a White slave master and his slave cook. The White slave master was married and had two sons by the White wife. He also kept my grandfather in his house and was raising him with his other sons. My grandfather's last name, complexion, and hair came from his father, the slave owner.

One day, my grandfather Namon, and one of his half-brothers had a little spat. The White wife told the slave owner, "If you don't beat that nigger, I will take my boys and leave."

Namon told his father, "If you do, I will run away."

I suppose the owner thought he couldn't run away because he was the son of a slave. Consequently, he whipped him. After everyone was asleep, my grandfather walked away. He kept going until he came to a place called Nashville, Arkansas. I think that's where he settled and, I guess, started farming. That's where he met and married a lady named Callie Marshall, the grandmother I never met. She passed away before my father and mother met.

The Beginning of My Lidfe: Happy Days

My parents: Arthur and Pearl Frierson

Namon and Callie had five children. My mother, Pearl, was the oldest. I don't know how they met, but my father, Arthur Frierson, asked my grandfather, Namon, if he could marry Pearl, my mother. My grandfather, Namon, finally brought my mother to Patmos, Arkansas. That's where they got their license and were married. Papa brought Mama to the farm and they made their home there.

My parents' first child was a boy, John Cecil. The second was Hayward, whom we called "Nap" because of his hair. The third was Cottrell. We called him "Cot." The fourth child was finally a girl named Clementine, called "Miss Clem." The fifth was Mance. He was the sick one, who suffered from epilepsy. The sixth and seventh were twins, Perry and Derry, who died four days after birth. The eighth was Ezekiel, called "Zeke." He was Mr. Pretty Boy. Then ninth was Frank, and he was the funny boy. Every day, he gave a comedy show at the house and we didn't have to pay for it. Now, can you believe that? The tenth child was Amanda named after Grandmother and we called her "Mandy." The eleventh child was Berneice, called "Bern." The twelfth child, Earnestine, we called "Earn." She was the scaredy-cat, afraid of everything. The thirteenth child was Eva Pearl, named after Mama. She was the pretty one with green eyes. I think we all wished we were more like her. The fourteenth was Mattie Mae, called "Mat." Now here came the fifteenth and the last child, me, the ugly duckling. My mama had run out of names when I got here. She could have taken my

The Beginning of My Lidfe: Happy Days

My family and Uncle Ezekiel's family.

brother's nickname, Nap, and called me Nappy. I'm sure she must have thought about that name for me for some time. Then, she finally said, "I'll name her Ojarva."

After my mother named me that, our teacher came to the house to see Mama. She asked my mother, "What did you name her?"

"Ojarva," Mama replied.

"What? Pearl, you can't name that child that. Where did you get that name? You've got to change it!"

"Myself," Mama said. "If you think it's that bad, you change it, because I'm not."

Now just think. If my name had remained Ojarva and, in 2008, we had a president named Obama, who knows? He might have invited me to the White House just because of my name. I didn't say he would have, but he might have, just to ask where I got that name from. It's so much like his. I could have said, "I really don't know, Mr. President. But do you think, just maybe, your grandfather's spirit could have touched my mother's spirit and gave it to her? You know, Mr. President, we might be long, long, long distant relatives." Ha, ha, ha!

Well, we could have had a good laugh with it, or given him another embarrassment that he could laugh at. Well, we all have our dreams, don't we?

Getting back to that darn teacher. Would you believe that woman went to Hope to the office where they kept the birth certificates? She told the woman, "I'm here because I'm changing Pearl's last child's name."

The woman asked, "To what?"

"I am changing it to Revoyda." The teacher sounded adamant.

Looking puzzled, the woman asked, "How do you spell that?"

"Re-voy-da," the teacher replied.

The woman just put a scratch over Ojarva and wrote in Revoyda. I'm sure the lady said, "That's worse," but she didn't care, so what? It's been a mess for me ever since I got it. In fact, that name has been a curse for me in my own family. My sisters call me "Vorda," my brothers call me "Re-V." Now, that's a mess.

It is hard when someone asks your name and you tell them and the next word is, "WHAT?" You must spell it, Re-voy-da, and say it again. That's the way it has been all of my life.

My family was a family of love. We played by ourselves, or with Uncle Ezekiel's children. By the time I was about four, my older brother was in high school. He made a mistake and got a girl pregnant. The young girl asked my mother if she would keep her baby until she could get a job. Naturally, my mother kept her. The baby was my brother's child. Mary Ellen was her name and we loved her very much. I considered her my baby sister.

I don't understand how Mama and Papa made it with all of us kids. Of course, the boys were there. As they grew older, they were a big help.

While we were growing up, Mama had asthma really bad. There were no inhalers back then. Sometimes she would have such bad attacks that my dad and brothers had to take her outside and walk her around the house for her to get oxygen into her lungs. I will never forget her last attack. It was so severe, we thought we would lose our mother. All the girls were in the bedroom, crying. The attack was so long and hard, it seemed like it would last forever. However, about 11:00 p.m. that night, God brought her out of it, and she never had another attack. Praise God.

We grew everything we ate. We grew lots of corn. We canned it, fed it to the animals, dried it out, and took it to the mill to grind for cornmeal. We also grew all kinds of vegetables. We had a peach orchard and had plenty of peaches. We owned cows, pigs, and mules. Zeke had a pretty horse named Bugger Red. He was a bad horse. In fact, no one could ride him, but Zeke. One day, he put me on that crazy horse and he started bucking. Zeke got me off before he could hurt me. He said the horse had to get used to my smell.

"Smell hell," I told Zeke. "Don't put me on that fool horse no more."

He just laughed.

We played games like hide-and-go-seek, baseball, horse ring, and racing. We didn't play basketball because we didn't have the ball or the hoop to throw it in. We even had a Chinese checkers board and were happy with what we had.

The Beginning of My Lidfe: Happy Days

As I got older, I was always with Mama. I learned how to quilt, sew, and cook. One day, my brother, Mance, had a seizure. I thought he was clowning around and I started laughing. Mama popped me on the head. "Don't you ever laugh at him like that because he is sick," she said. Mama explained his condition to me, so I started spending more time with him.

As he grew up, Mance loved fishing. He would dig the worms from the dirt for bait, put them on the hook, and catch lots of fish.

One day, when Mance was about twenty-one years of age, he went fishing alone. I didn't see him anywhere so I went looking for him in the barn and didn't see him there. I thought, *He must have gone fishing.* I ran to the pond and there he was. Apparently, he had suffered a seizure, had fallen into the pond, and drowned. Naturally, I went running to the field to tell the family to come and get Mance. They all came running, but it was too late.

For a long time, I felt guilty because I was on the porch with Mary Ellen, and Mance was there for a while. I didn't see him leave, so I was not with him. Maybe I could have saved him or gotten to the family sooner. That didn't happen. Instead, we lost a dear brother. I still remember that day as if it were yesterday.

In Arkansas, everyone raised watermelons. We also had a black walnut tree in the field, with walnuts on the ground; we would collect them and put them in a homemade wooden box. In the back yard, when Mama was tired and did not feel like cooking, we ate melons or black walnuts for supper. We would bust the melons open, eat the center, and feed the rest to the pigs.

My sister, Mat, would always say, "Voyda, this watermelon."

"Slick," I would say, and then throw it to the pigs and burst another one.

Mat always did that until I would burst her one, taste it, and give it to her.

In Arkansas, the watermelon was very important to families in the forties. I believe that is when the Watermelon Festival began. The first festival, my daddy raised the second-largest round watermelon. I was very young and we did not go to the festival. My father would take the watermelon to the festival and, unfortunately, didn't bring it back. We didn't get to eat that one. I do remember when I went to my first and last festival. We made a trip from California to Hope, Arkansas. Later, my brother, Ezekiel, my sisters Bernice, Mattie and Eva Pearl, and her husband, all met in Hope, and headed off to the Watermelon Festival. Boy, those were some big, sweet watermelons. They were the largest I have ever seen, or ever *will* see. They were the best. There were two kinds. There were the round ones like my daddy won with. He also grew the long ones, but those things were so long, you couldn't carry them. All you could get was a slice to eat.

On this trip, we decided to get us a long slice of the watermelon, they would cut it down the middle so you would have 2 sides and each side was cut in half again. Then, that would get cut again. It was so hot down there; we struggled to eat that slice.

Brother Ezekiel said, "Hell, let's go. It's too hot out here and nobody can eat this much watermelon." Ha, ha, ha!

Now, if you have never been to the Hope Arkansas Watermelon Festival, you ought to go. They have the sweetest, biggest watermelons in the world.

Christmas was a very special time for us little girls. I guess my mother, father, and older brothers saved the whole year, penny by penny, to make sure Christmas was something very special and beautiful for us. Our brothers were determined to make us little girls truly believe in Santa Claus. We had no pictures of Santa Claus. We had no live man dressed in red to sit on his lap and tell him what we wanted. No, we had none of that. They just told us he won't come if you don't believe in Santa Claus because he won't think of you. We truly believed that. What they said, as far as we were concerned, was like gospel. Santa Claus could fly, had a sled, and drove flying reindeer.

On the night before Christmas, my brother, Cot, would say, "You little girls better get in that tub to take your bath, put on your gowns, and go to sleep. Do you hear me? Santa doesn't like being seen and he definitely doesn't like hardheaded little girls."

You better believe me; we did just what he told us to do. We were asleep after dark.

My mother would still have a couple of cakes to make. Cot and Nap would take their fingers and sop the bowl. When they were sure we were asleep, they would make sled marks and reindeer hooves, then drop candy all over the roof. They told us that the reindeer and sled stayed on the housetop, but Santa came down the chimney. He would fill our stockings with candy, apples, and oranges. Each one of us girls got a gift and then Santa would take two pieces of cake for himself and go back up the chimney to his sled. He then went to both Uncle Ezekiel's and Uncle Calvin's houses, leaving candy and suckers. He'd leave a track to each house. Oh, what a joy that day was! Each child had his or her own special gift. It was that way every Christmas for a few years.

My father had purchased twenty more acres of land and had just about paid for it. His friend, Attorney Robert Legrones, had found another forty acres of land with lots of timber and good hunting grounds. He was willing to sell it to Papa for $25.00. The arrangement was that my father would pay as he could, when he could. When Papa paid it off, it would be his land. Attorney Legrones and his wife signed on as backers for Papa. No matter how many bad White people there are, there's always a good one somewhere, and Attorney Legrones was Papa's good friend. Now, you have to understand that in those days it was very hard for Black folks to buy land. Black people were still very poor, picking cotton, and having to listen to the White man. So, why did Attorney

Legrones help Papa own land, and even vote? Because it was said all over the countryside, "Everybody loves Arthur." Yes, I'll never forget that. Everybody did love my Papa.

One day, my brother, Hayward, got really sick. Papa had to take him to the doctor. We had a Black doctor named Dr. Lewis who had graduated from Howard University Medical School. He said Hayward had to go to Hope Hospital because he had appendicitis. Now, in those days, the hospitals were in the White section, with only a few beds segregated for Blacks, and we were all scared. The next day, Papa went back to Hope to get Hayward and they had already given him the surgery. He had appendicitis and Papa said he would not be out soon. His appendix had ruptured and he spent a month in the hospital. That is a fact. When the doctors discharged Hayward, it was so good to finally have him back home.

Now, I know you all remember that President Bill Clinton comes from Hope, Arkansas. Well, did you know that his mother was a nurse in that very hospital? Yes, she was and she gave me a shot one time, and my very first dose of Advil, to kill the pain from a dog bite.

The War

Growing up, my family was so close, but then came World War II. That war destroyed my family. When the war first started, they weren't taking Black men. After a while, the war got so bad, they started enlisting Black men. My two brothers, Hayward and Cottrell, were two of the first Blacks to volunteer to join. They went to Fort Bragg, North Carolina, I think.

My older brother, John, was in Howard University, an all Black college in Washington, DC. My older sister, Clem, had gone to Tuskegee Institute in Alabama. Back on the farm, Mama, Papa, Zeke, Frank, and us girls continued living and working the farm. We were making it okay, all working in the fields, picking cotton. Mama would pick two rows at a time. I picked the third row next to her, but the one who could not keep up was Earn, Scaredy-Cat, as we called her. Everyone was keeping up but her. Mama looked back, saw her, and told me to go back and help her catch up. She'd keep my row up with hers.

So, I went back to her and she was picking one-quarter of a bow of cotton at a time and looking for sting worms. I told her, "Stop that, pick the whole bow of cotton." She was still acting stupid, but I got her caught up and put her ahead of everyone. Then I went back to my row.

Mama and Papa were strict on raising us. If you didn't do what they told you, you might get a whipping. I was always a little hardheaded. You had to get your own switch. One time, I think it was Bern who told me to get a big switch because it would break quicker. Stupid me! I did just what she said. Ha! Ha!

Mama said, "Oh, you brought me a big one."

Under my breath, I mumbled, "Aww shit."

The first hit, the switch broke, but Mama took the ends and gave me a good whipping anyway.

I went to Bern. "You told me wrong," I said, rubbing my behind. "You knew better."

"It broke, didn't it?" Bern quipped.

"Yes."

"Then I was right. I said it would break." Ha, Ha, Ha

I thought about it. "I'm not going to get that one anymore. I'm going to get a tiny one."

"Well, as you say, you do," said Bern.

Well, I did that the next time I was due for a whipping.

Mama looked down at the tiny switch. "Oh, a tiny one this time. Drop your drawers." Mama laughed.

"Oh, Lord," I said,

It was just skin and that little switch. She did her thing.

The next time I got a whipping, it was from Papa. He thought you could just stand there and take anything. I had gotten a long splinter in my hand and he started picking it out. I started pulling my hand away from him. He popped me on the butt with something and it started to bleed. Mama popped him on the nose.

"Chick, you are spoiling these girls," Papa said. "They can't take nothing, especially that one." He meant me.

"Well, you are not going to hurt her. She's just a child."

He walked away. Mama put some iodine on my hand and wrapped it up. She said in three days, there would be pus around the splinter, then I can open it up, be able to push all the pus and the splinter out. It happened just like she said. She also redressed my cut and said it would be well soon.

I got in trouble again with Papa. All he said was, "Get away from me. You're hardheaded and you can't take anything. You ain't mine no ways."

I said, "I am the only one that is yours, Papa, because I'm the fool in the family—just like you."

Mama hollered with laughter and he did, too.

Mama said, "Well, she got you that time, Dad."

From that time on, for some reason, I became his pal.

That war was still going on. They drafted my older brother, John, out of college. That darn war was getting worse and I didn't even know where our brothers were going. Because of the war, there was a lot of extra work in other states. Papa went away to work for a while, too. We knew they would eventually draft Zeke, and the government did. Even the horse, Bugger Red, was sad. He would let you pet him and Frank would ride him sometimes. He rode him to the highway to the mailbox to get the mail. Everyone was sending a little money and Mama was paying the bills. Over time, she paid off the land. Attorney Legrones sent her the deed to the forty acres. As long as we had Funny Boy and Mary Ellen, everything was fine.

The Beginning of My Lidfe: Happy Days

We had relatives, the Straughters and the Forbes, that lived down in some part of the country, but we would only see them when we would go to church on Sunday.

Well, it was just us girls, Mama, and Frank left at home. We worked on the farm. For some reason, cucumbers started selling, so Mama decided to raise them. That was hard work. They paid more for the little ones and that made it hard. They grew so fast, you had to pick them every day, in the morning, to get the good ones. We were so glad when the cucumber season was over, but then it was time to plant something else.

I bet you can't guess what was fixing to happen. They were going to draft my baby brother, Funny Boy, in that war! Everybody was crying and he was, too. What could they do with a little boy like Frank? Mama had to write to Papa to come home to help her calm the kids. Well, he did. Those people, darn it, still took Frank and put him in the Navy. They were fixing to send Hayward overseas, but, for some reason, they were not sending Cot. Now they had always been together. What the heck was going on?

They had written a letter to Mama saying that Cot had a hole in his heart and they were discharging him. What was going on? He didn't have a hole in his heart before he left—not that we knew of. Well, they were giving him an honorable discharge. Not that it mattered to me, I was just glad he was out. They were also giving him some kind of government letter, stating that when, or wherever, he got a job, he could not be fired. That was good! Cot was coming home to see us, but he was not coming to stay. He was going to San Francisco, California. My father was also going to San Francisco to work at the shipyard.

Then it was just Mama and us girls left at home. One day, Mary Ellen's mama was coming. She was married and had come to get her baby, my little sister. Again, we all started our crying fits.

"Mama, you can't let her take our baby sister," I protested.

"She's her mother and I can't keep a child from its mother," Mama said. "She's John's baby, too, and I'm her grandmother, but she must go."

We cried, but we had to let her go, so our little sister was gone.

Only Mama and the five of us girls remained on the farm, even Amanda, who would be going to high school in Hope, living with Mrs. Louis. If Papa was able, when she finished high school, she was planning to go to A M & N College in Pine Bluff, Arkansas, which is now the University of Arkansas at Pine Bluff. That would be another loss.

For a couple of years, it had been just Mama and us five girls. We had to work hard on the farm, but I think the war was about over. My brothers and Papa would be coming home, but my brothers wouldn't be staying. No one was staying, but Papa. Frank came home on furlough for two weeks, but he was going back to the ship, which was docked in California. It seemed like all my brothers were going back to that place. I wondered, *Why?*

High School and Hope

Now, in the winter, it would be time for me and the last four girls to go to high school. I knew nobody would keep five country girls. I asked Papa if I would have to drive us to school every day. He said, "Don't worry about it. Just do your work."

When all the boys were in the service, Mama sold Bugger Red, the horse. I loved that old horse. I couldn't ride him, but he was so pretty. Now, it was almost September, almost time to start school. Our parents packed us up, put us in the truck, then took us to Hope. They drove up to a little white house right behind Yerger High School.

He told us, "This is where you will be staying."

Oh! My dear, God! They have made my daddy rich, I thought.

Our parents told us we had better study our lessons and be good girls because people would be watching out for us for them.

When school opened, somebody had the gall to ask me if I was from the country.

I told them, "You bet I am. That's where the money comes from. Of course, what you don't know can't hurt you, can it?"

I wondered why he asked such a stupid question in the first place. Naturally, I didn't tell them how hard you had to work for that money. I just thought my dad was rich.

We had been in school for a while and I decided I wanted some candy. So, I went up to the Checkers Café & Pharmacy and asked the girl for a Baby Ruth candy bar. I told her to put it on my daddy's bill.

"Who is your daddy?" she asked.

"Arthur Frierson," I replied. I wondered why she asked me who my daddy was. Well, he had a bill there, so she put the candy on his bill. I left with my candy.

Time passed and I went to get my candy. In fact, I kept doing it until one day I walked in and that pharmacist was there to meet me.

"Revoyda," he said, "you have been coming in here, putting this candy on Arthur's bill. From now on, I'm making you a bill of your own and you will pay for it. Now, you sign here and go get yourself a little job. Now go on home and get your lessons."

Oh, shit! *We are not rich and everyone is watching us, darn.* That old man scared me almost crazy. *What kind of job am I going to get?*

I believe it was that old pharmacist that told two old White women to let me work for them after school. I only had to work on Monday, Wednesday, and Friday. I would clean their house on Monday and Wednesday. On Friday, I would clean the little room at the church where they kept the children and taught them Sunday School. They were regular teachers for Hope's White school. I had been working for them for about three months. I could get all the candy that my sisters and I wanted, could eat, or wanted to eat, during our study.

When I was fourteen, there was an old White man who started sitting on his porch, waiting for me to finish work and go home. He first started whistling at me. I would speed up my steps, but one day, he got in his old car and chased me all the way across the railroad tracks to our section of town. I was so tired and scared. It was Friday and Mama would be there on Saturday. I would tell her what was happening.

Mama was there on Saturday, as usual, and I told her what had happened. She told me to tell the ladies that I would have to quit. On Monday, I normally worked for about one hour and was gone before they got home. But I waited until the older lady got home and told her I had to quit working for them. She asked why. I told her what the old man had done.

"No, you are not quitting." She took me by the hand. "Come with me."

We went over to that old man's house. He started to go into the house. I was scared as hell. She told him, "Wait. You see me coming. This little girl is my helper and you had better leave her alone. Do you hear me? You had better stay out of that tacky old car, following her, or I'm going to have you arrested." She looked at me and said, "If he ever bothers you again, tell me."

"Yes, Ma'am," I said.

Now, we lived on our side of town, and they lived on theirs, but lots of Black women and girls went to the White side of town to work in the households, to cook, clean, and raise White children. Were we afraid? Well, it was just what we did. My experience with that old White man wasn't uncommon, but it made me mindful. We all knew that the White man could do whatever he wanted. The only way to protect myself was to run, so that's what I done, but I knew I was lucky that those women I worked for liked me enough to watch out for me.

That old man must have been scared of her because he never bothered me again. At least, he stayed on the porch. He would whistle really softly, every now and then.

The teachers paid me $1.00 a day. I could get what I wanted. They also had a layaway plan back in those days at the dress shop. I was doing okay. I could put a dollar on a dress for me, or any of my sisters, and pay it off in a week or two.

My sister, Eva, had a close friend named Nona Jean. The three of us became a trio at school. People expected us to be in every program we had at the school. One year, Mrs. Naomi got an old play called "Polly, Put the Kettle On and We'll All Have Tea."

Mrs. Naomi chose me for the role of Polly. I must have played the part pretty well because we did it three times at our school. Then we did it at the White school. The place was full, but we had to go through the back door. Can you imagine the stars of the play, having to go through the back door? Ha, ha, ha! But that's the way it was in those days.

Not good. Still, not good.

One day, Mary Tennessee and I were practicing ball. Mary Tennessee and her sister were great ballplayers. They were just before their time. Since Mary and I were so close, I was on the team even though I could not play. My sister, Mat, came crying to me. She said a boy had hit her.

"Which one?" I asked.

We ran back to where he was.

She pointed her finger at a boy about my size. "That one."

I just walked up to him, popped him in the nose and it started to bleed.

"Don't you ever mess with my sister," I said.

The other boys told me I was a crazy, stupid, country girl.

"Just like you," I said. "We are all country."

I went back to my friend, Mary, who was trying to teach me how to make a basket. I never was good at it.

Later, our old principal, Mr. Harris, died. We got a new one named Mr. Rutherford. He had three little kids. Would you believe soon after he got there, he married Mrs. Harris, of all people? She had no kids, wanted no kids, and was always gone.

The next year, Mr. Rutherford found out I was working for those two White women, so he asked me if I would work for him instead, taking care of his kids after school. He would pay me $5.00 a week. I thought that was good. I asked Mama and she talked to him. I worked the summer for the ladies and told them I would start working for my principal when school started. They wished me good luck and said they hated to lose me. It was nice of them to say that, and I would miss working for them, too. They were old maids and had been good to me.

I began working for Mr. Rutherford when school began. I would feed his kids, check their homework, give them a bath, get them ready for bed, then leave. In the morning, I would give them their breakfast (naturally, I ate something, too) and helped them get ready for school. Everything was going okay until Mr. Rutherford started teaching a veteran's class after school. He wanted me to stay with his kids until he got home.

The classes were for the returned veterans who had not finished school before going into the service, just like my baby brother, Frank. It was a good thing, but it started after we were out of school. In fact, the classes went from 5:00 p.m. to 8:00 p.m. He would turn off all the lights around the school and then come home. I had to go home in the dark, get my lessons, get up in the morning, go to his house, feed his kids, go back home and get myself ready for school. I started being a little late for school, myself.

The school had a policy that if you were late more than once, you must have an excuse from a parent. My second time to be late

The Beginning of My Lidfe: Happy Days

was for Mrs. Naomi's history class. It was Negro History and I had been late two days in a row. She said I had to have an excuse and I told her I would get one.

I went to Mr. Rutherford's office for an excuse because he was the reason for my tardiness. He told me the excuse had to come from my parents. I told him he was the reason I was late for class because I was taking care of his kids, and tomorrow I would get an excuse from my parents, but he owed me an excuse for today. He gave me the excuse and I went back to class.

When my mother came on Saturday, I told her what had happened.

"Where does Mr. Rutherford live?" she asked.

"In the Harris home."

It seemed like within the blink of an eye, we were knocking on the door. Mr. Rutherford answered it.

"Are you Professor Rutherford?"

"Yes."

"I am Pearl Frierson. The child beside me is my baby and we have a few things to clear up. Now, we can stand in the door and do this here on the porch, clear and clean, or you can be a man and invite us inside to do it quietly."

"Please, Mrs. Frierson, come in and have a seat on the couch." He opened the door and we followed him inside to the living room. We both sat down.

Mama started talking. "This is my baby child, just like your children are yours. When you asked my child to come here after school, she didn't come to be a mother. The agreement was she would leave school, come here, feed your kids, check their homework to make sure it was done, bathe them and get them ready for bed. All this is to be done before night and way before the lights are turned off around that school. That way she can get her homework done, take her bath, get in her bed and get some rest. She goes to school, too, you know.

"The next morning, she will be able to get here, feed your children and check that they are ready for school. Then she can go home, get herself ready and be at school on time. Knowing my kids as I do, Revoyda can do that in an hour or less and be at school on time herself.

"There will be no new changing of the agreement because you need extra help. If you do, you need a housekeeper, not another child. I expect you to be responsible for any excuses she needs pertaining to this job. Do we agree?"

"Yes, ma'am."

"Do you understand, Revoyda, that I do not expect you to be late for school?"

"Yes, ma'am."

"Now if you and I are not in agreement with this, say so now. If it is no, we will leave now, and I mean right now."

"Yes, ma'am. Yes, ma'am, I agree with that."

My mother told him she was at home in the country during the week. She continued, "I know, and I expect my baby to be at my home here on time and at school on time."

I worked for him for about two more years. Everything was fine from that day on.

Thinking About the Past and Looking Toward the Future

When I finished high school, I got a scholarship to Philander Smith College in Little Rock, Arkansas. I didn't know why I got the scholarship. I was not just a worker, but I worked the whole time I was in high school. I was not a total dummy either. I studied and did not flunk tests. There was only one girl who was better than I was. Her name was Hazel Bradley and she was the top student. She was the valedictorian of the class and I was the number two student in my class. They called me the salutatorian. I didn't know what that meant, but I was well known and got the scholarship.

There were the two of us left at home, Mattie and me. I was thinking, *what are we going to do?* I didn't want to go to Little Rock without Mattie, so I was thinking maybe we should go into the Army.

I told Mama and asked her if she thought that was a good idea. She told me to wait until she wrote to Hayward to see what he had to say. The answer came back from him. He said, "No, they are not going into the Army. You keep them right there until I can get some leave time from my work. Then I will come and take them to San Francisco to live with Cot and both can go to school there."

Well, we were waiting for Nap. Raised together all of our lives, it was now time we were fixing to separate from our mother and father. I was wondering what it would feel like not to see them, or not to be able to see them. I was now becoming an older girl. Mama had been there all my life. Now to go to California, what would I do?

I took a walk in the park, but Mary Tennessee was not there. No one was there but me. I was just sitting there, thinking about leaving. We had enjoyed our life, but what would tomorrow bring? I was thinking of the past. It was time I started thinking of the future. I was thinking of my mother's good cooking, what a strong woman she was, and what a good life she'd made for us. What was I going to gain by leaving?

When I came from the park, I told my mom what I had been thinking. She told me it was a joy for them to have raised all their children. It was a blessing from God, but it was now time for us to take the blessing that God was giving us and use it to our best ability. "Dad and I will be fine."

She said they would be living in town sometimes. "We have lots of relatives in town." They would be going to the farmhouse and still grow vegetables and fruits, and what they need and want to grow. "Not what we have to anymore, but what we want to," Mama added. That made me realize they had done their job, and now it was time for me to do mine.

In a few weeks, Hayward came home. In those days, we could not use just any hotels, toilets, or water fountains. Sometimes, they had signs for colored people's water fountains, but not often. There was supposed to be something called The Green Book that listed hotels and motels that allowed colored people, but we didn't have one of them. All you could get without any trouble, just like everybody else, was gas.

When we left for California, Mama had cooked chicken, made peanut butter and jelly sandwiches, and used some of her large jars to fill with water. Mama also gave us some of the quilts she had made. I had helped her with some of those quilts. We said goodbye to Mama and Papa. They told us to be good girls. That was the worst moment of my life because we were leaving them alone.

During our trip to California, Hayward would sleep in the grass on the side of the highway. It was such a long trip. There were no freeways, just two-lane highways. I thought we would never get out of Texas. My brother was so tired. It seemed like it took days to get there. When we finally arrived in Los Angeles, California, we got to see our sister, Earnestine (Scaredy-Cat) and brother, Ezekiel.

Mattie and I stayed there for about four days, so Hayward could get some real sleep.

Now, we would be on our way to San Francisco. That was a long day's journey. We would be staying at Cot's house. We had not seen Cot since he left the service. I think that was a new experience for him and for us. He had been by himself for years.

So, it was new for all of us. Hayward spent the night at Cot's and got some more rest, and the next day, he left to go back to Los Angeles. Now we were where we would be living with Cot.

The Beginning of My Lidfe: Happy Days

My brother Frank in his Navy uniform.

My brother Cot.

The Beginning of My Lidfe: Happy Days

My oldest brother, John, graduating from Howard University.

Me with my sisters.

My husband Bill (left) with my sisters husbands.

The Beginning of My Lidfe: Happy Days

Me with my brothers and sisters.

PART TWO
Starting College and Turning Pro

From Revoyda to Ketty

We made it to Cot's house, an old two-story house. It had two bedrooms on the second floor. Cot's room was downstairs. Mattie thought the house was haunted and wanted to sleep with me. That was okay. We had been sleeping that way all of our lives.

I would think about Mama and Papa. As usual, I was doing the cooking for us. I would have something for Cottrell to eat when he got home from work. It seemed as if he had never had a home-cooked meal. It was just the three of us, and I thought of how Mama used to cook for us, twice a day. There were times when she would make special things on Sunday, like bread pudding. Then there was a butter roll. She made cookies called tea cakes and, of course, she made the best peach cobblers because she put lots of peaches and not a lot of bread in it. Not like the peach cobblers of today, which are bread puddings with canned peaches.

Starting College and Turning Pro

After we got to California, it seemed as if I had become the oldest and had to do what I needed to take over the house…and them. To me, life had changed altogether. Everything was different. It seemed as if Cottrell was even different. My responsibilities had even changed. I guess it had to be because we were older. We had been away from our brother for so long since his discharge from the Army, we had to learn each other's ways all over again.

On Sunday, we would go to church. I joined the choir. Our rehearsals were on Thursday evening. Mat said that the old woman who used to live in Cot's house would blow in her ear. I don't know if that old woman died in that house or what, but she only bothered me one time when I was going down the stairs. It seemed like I felt something. I told her if she followed me again, I would kick her butt down those stairs. I never felt anything afterward. I guess she didn't know that you can't kick what you can't see, but she had given Mat a hard time, though. I was sorry about that, but one couldn't fight what they couldn't feel or see either.

It was getting close to September and Cot had checked the schools. He knew the date we had to start, and that we also had to take a bus ride to school. Cot had given us his rules—go to church, go to school, and no babies. That was great for me. Boys didn't like me no way. I easily lived by that rule.

It was time to go to school. We would go to City College, San Francisco. Cot said, "Do what I say and you will have money, clothing, food, and a place to stay as long as you want. But please. No babies."

Now, you may wonder how I started to call myself Ketty. Well, it happened on the first day of college. We took the bus and went up the hill to the main building. All of a sudden, a young boy walked up to me, of all people.

"Hi. Is this your first day of school?"

"Yes," I said.

"Me, too. I'm excited. Are you?"

"No, I'm scared."

"My name is Robert. What is your name?"

"Revoyda." Well, here came the big question.

"What?"

Then I started thinking. The first thing that came into my mind was a kitten. But the way I spelled and said 'kitty' came out sounding like 'Ketty.' So, I answered, "Just call me Ketty."

"Ketty? Okay, Ketty, but that other name was kinda weird."

"I know, Robert."

"Come on, Mat." I sped up my walk.

I heard Robert say to another boy, "She's kinda cute, but country."

"Did you hear what that nut said?" I asked Mat. "I should go back there and tell him off or knock his butt off."

"No, Voyda, you are not going to start that stuff here," Mat said. "You are going to straighten up and let's do what we are supposed to do."

That was the shock of my life. It was the first time Mat had ever spoken up to me.

"What is wrong with you, Mat?"

"Voyda, just shut up."

I was so shocked; I could have peed on myself and never felt the water. Someone would have to tell me, "Girl, you're wet. You better go to the toilet." Ha, Ha, Ha!

Well, I had decided that I was going to study nursing. My next challenge was meeting with my counselor. I told her what I wanted to study. She didn't give me any counseling, just English, History, and Math classes. She told me I had to take three science classes in nursing. She started naming them off with one called Science 1A. It had a 1 and an A. I thought it must have been the first class, so I said I'll take the 1A. She gave me my schedule and told me where to get my books.

Well, everything was going okay, except that Science 1A. I made an F on every test. I spoke to a White girl classmate. "I'm failing this class."

"Drop it before you fail the class."

I asked how to drop a class mid semester and she told me to go to my counselor and tell her I wanted to drop the class.

I said to myself, "*Don't tell me I have to go back to this heifer this soon.*" I had to, and I did.

I didn't want to go to Cot and tell him I was dropping a class, so as I was walking down the hall, I met a boy, asked him if this school had music classes.

He said, "Yes."

It turned out they had a nice choir and a director named Dr. Huns. The boy told me where it was located. I went to the building and met the director, who was very nice. I had been singing all my life in school and church.

So, when we met, Dr. Huns asked, "So you want to sing in the choir?"

"Yes, I do."

"What voice do you sing?"

"What do you need?"

We both laughed.

"I'm going to start you with the sopranos. Anybody with that much confidence must be a soprano."

"I can sing bass, too, if you need it."

"Be here tomorrow at three," he said.

I had been with the choir at Second Church since we started going to church in San Francisco. The pianist at the church asked if I wanted to take voice lessons. I really didn't know what she was talking about. When it comes to voice, you either can sing, or you can't.

"You have a beautiful voice and about a three-octave range."

I knew what octaves were because I had studied piano lessons in Hope with Mrs. Lewis.

When it came to voice lessons, I said I had no money and couldn't pay for lessons.

"Did I ask you for money, Revoyda?"

"No."

Thus, we started voice lessons. The first song, of course, was "The Lord's Prayer." She taught me many songs, but the first in a different language was naturally "Ava Maria." I still have it.

I really didn't know what it was going to be like, voice lessons. But after a few times, I understood what she was making me do. There were exercises for the voice. There was "me, me, me, me." There was "ar, ar, ar, ar." There were exercises to make your voice go high and to warm up your voice.

At school, if Dr. Huns wanted something special done vocally, he would say, "Do you think you can make that?" I would always say yes.

For the next semester, I went to that counselor and got my classes. I always was stupid and got that Science 1A, but I stayed with the choir. Everything was fine, but, as usual, I had to drop that class again. Finally, my voice teacher at the church got someone to help with that Science class during the summer.

The next semester, I was doing okay. Not too good. Still with the Science 1A, but I was passing with low grades.

During one choir practice, there was a man from the University of California in Berkeley, Music Department. He said they always had a show during the summer. He asked Dr. Huns if he had someone he thought would be good and would like to do the show with them.

Dr. Huns said, "Yes." He pointed at me and asked if I would like to do it.

"I don't care." I shrugged. I thought I was doing it for the choir. The teacher from the university gave me a piece of paper with where and when they would start rehearsing, how I would get there and how long the show would be going on during the summer.

I finally passed my Science 1A with a C, which was passing back in my day. Of course, that's because a little White boy had helped me all that semester.

We started the show. I would take the bus across the Bay Bridge to a place in Oakland. When the show started, I met the manager or owner of The Purple Onion. He asked me if I wanted to go professional.

"No, I am studying nursing and want to be a nurse." He gave me his card and said if I changed my mind and wanted to go professional, call him.

After the show closed and I was home with my sister, I found out she had a boyfriend. One day when I came home, this man was getting in his car. I asked my sister who he was and she said, "My friend."

"Leave that nut alone. He doesn't look right to me."

She didn't seem to understand what I was saying. Mat was tired of staying at the school, waiting for me. The boy used that as an excuse to bring her home. It was like talking to the moon.

From Co-Ed to Club Girl

After a while, Mat and Cot started to have problems with each other. I guess Mattie was having trouble following Cottrell's rules. We were going to have to get out of that old haunted house. Consequently, I went to Hunter Point on the hill and was able to get a one-bedroom apartment. Now I would have to get a job. Cot paid two month's rent and gave us money for food. I went to the post office. I thought they would hire me because Mat and I worked there before. They allowed students to work there during the Christmas season. I knew how to do it. You had to separate the states by states and the city by city. You had to separate whether it was going by air or regular. I thought since I had told them I had worked there before they would be a little bit more considerate of what I knew, but "no hire." I went to the shipyard, "no hire." I also

Purple Onion in San Francisco, California

Maya Angelou and me during our Purple Onion days in San Francisco, California.

Starting College and Turning Pro

went downtown to the stores and thought they would hire me as a sweeper, but "no hire."

I remembered the card and I called the man at The Purple Onion in San Francisco. I told him who I was and where I met him. He remembered me.

He said, "Oh, you decided to go pro."

"I need a job. Is the offer still open?"

"When do you want to start?"

"Today, if the offer is open."

"No, come on Monday at 8:00 p.m."

I was so glad; it was a job and that was all that mattered. So, I started on March 7, 1955, and on that same night, Phyllis Diller started her show business career. Back then, things were different for all women, Black and White. In those days, you didn't see a lot of women doing stand-up comedy. Do you know who the star was? It was another door opener, Maya Angelou. Of course, then she wasn't Dr. Maya Angelou, the Poet Laureate, playwright, and actress. She was a bad Calypso singer who said she was from Jamaica, and I was so excited to see someone from "another country."

The owner told me the first show was at 8:00 p.m., and I would be the opening act. Phyllis would be the second act, the comedian. She did look funny, but people did not laugh at her jokes that night. I was a little confused. When Maya came on, I realized why the place was so full. Maya was a talent in her own right. I liked the way she dressed. She wore leotards under a long dress, slit up to the hip and didn't wear any shoes. She sang what she said were Jamaican songs and did some kind of dance, and to me, it was good. Boy, I wanted to sing some of those Jamaican songs she was singing. We had been there for a couple of weeks. I wanted to meet her, but I was not an outgoing person.

One day, I just felt like I had to introduce myself. I went to her dressing room. "Miss Angelou, I'm Ketty and I wanted to meet you. It is such a pleasure to see someone from another country."

Maya started laughing at me so hard, I got mad.

"Are you laughing at me?"

"Girl, I'm from Arkansas, just like you."

"No, no, no. You're from Jamaica."

"Do you know where Stamps is?"

"Stamps where?"

"Arkansas."

"That place is smaller than Hope. How dare you do this to me, girl?"

We both laughed uncontrollably. We spent a lot of time together. I made a joke about Stamps. "Stamps doesn't even have a railroad station. At least Hope had a station and the high school was the first Black high school built west of the Mississippi River." I asked her if Stamps had a high school and we laughed.

She knew I didn't know much about the business, so she introduced me to other entertainers at The Hungry Eye. The Hungry Eye was across the street from The Purple Onion, and I guess you could call it a Folk Club. I met a trio there called Peter, Paul, and Mary, who would become one of the most important Folk acts of the 60s. I also met the Smothers Brothers who would go on to have two television shows, protest the Vietnam War, and challenge racism and TV censorship. Even though Folk music was a whole lot different than what I did, I liked them very much.

Maya was a good friend. I asked her where she got her songs and she told me she made them up as she went along. I said, "Well, you'd better get ready to make up more because Phyllis is about through with her show." One night, Sammy Davis Jr. came to the show to see Maya, and I met him. Now I know I do not have to tell you who he was; a man of many talents—singer, musician, dancer, actor, vaudevillian, comedian and activist known for his impressions of actors, musicians, and other celebrities. Sammy was one of the most talented men in show business. The night I met him, he told me I had a nice voice and took a picture with me.

It was the last show and I told Maya I would see her tomorrow. We had been working for quite some time.

I caught the bus after the last show. I had to walk about three blocks from 3rd Street and up a long staircase to get to the apartment. That night when I got home, Mattie was in a panic because she had to go to the hospital. We made it down to Cot's house, and he got up and took us. She had to stay there for a while so, I would stay at the hospital each night. I would leave the hospital at three o'clock in the afternoon, get something to eat, and lay down for a few minutes. At six o'clock in the evening, I would get ready for work, catch the bus at seven o'clock and would be at work by eight o'clock. It was a hard five days. That was my schedule the whole time she was in the hospital.

Because of Mattie's troubles, we had to go it alone. I had to find work right away so that we could afford our own place, since we could no longer live with our brother. During her time in the hospital, and just after, I had to take on a lot of responsibility by earning money for the both of us, and looking after her, too, but this also helped Mattie grow and become more independent. All of this may sound like was a difficult road, but it's that road that led me to show business.

Yes, it was good because it got Mat out of that haunted house, and away from that old woman who always seemed to whisper in her ear, and it got me into a profession that I never thought I would be in.

At the club, I met a man named Fredrick Maxwell, who owned an art gallery in San Francisco called Maxwell Galleries. He sent painters and other artists to Europe to study their craft. There were three of them at that time. When they came back to the States, he wanted to see if their art had improved after their stay in Europe. He asked them to do different paintings of me. One was a painter and two were sculptors. The painter did a painting of me; I still have it. The two sculptors did two different busts of me that Mr. Maxwell gave to me.

I worked with Phyllis and Maya for at least a year. It was nice to be talking to Maya again at the club, but they were talking about opening a new Purple Onion in Los Angeles. That's kind of strange. They wanted me to be the singer to open the club there. I felt I was too inexperienced to open a club by myself. There were no comedians, just the jazz trio and me. If I left San Francisco, what would I have done with Mat? She would be alone with nobody but Cot, and he could not take care of her.

I wouldn't have to worry for long, because my sister, Amanda, had gotten married and they moved to San Francisco. Berniece and her husband had separated. She had two children and she left them with Mama in Hope. She was a beautician. When Berniece came to San Francisco, she would be with Mat. It was good for Mat and me to have our sisters with us. That was a relief for me. I think my brother, Frank, had left the ship and was in Los Angeles. So, I planned to be with Frank, Ezekiel, Hayward, and Earnestine when The Purple Onion opened in Los Angeles.

Los Angeles, Stars, and Very Fine Gowns

I had spent the year with Maya and Phyllis at the Purple Onion in San Francisco. After some time, the new club had opened and I was in Los Angeles. Things were going all right. I had been there for a while, and would you believe Maya showed up? It was nice to see her and I don't know why they didn't have me and Maya open the club together. It would have been better. Maybe my brother, Frank, could have been the comic.

Maya had started writing. She was no longer singing.

I was enjoying Los Angeles because Frank and Earn were there. I was going all the time. Earnestine had a little car and a little dog named Rugie. Every time I would go out, I'd tell Rugie, "Let's go," and he would come. One day, I think Rugie got a little tired, so I took him home and gave him some water. Rugie got under the bed. It was getting close to the time I had to pick up Earnestine from work. Rugie was still under the bed and wouldn't come out.

This time when I said, "Come on, Rugie," he started whining and backed up under the bed. Ha, Ha, Ha.

I said it again and Frank told me, "Leave that dog alone. You go so damn much; you'll make a dog tired. Just go and get Earn." He started mumbling to himself.

I said to myself, *I didn't come down here to get a dog tired and my brother, Frank, talking to himself. I'd better slow down.* I picked up Earnestine and told her what had happened.

She cracked up and said, "Well, you learned something today, didn't you?"

Groucho Marx came to The Purple Onion (Los Angeles) and asked if I wanted to do his television show, *You Bet Your Life*. I had never been on one before and, as usual, I said, "I don't care." So, Groucho gave me my first appearance on television. That was in 1957. I appeared on that show as Ketty Frierson.

That same year I became the first Black woman since Josephine Baker, to be featured in The Ziegfeld Follies. I performed two numbers, "It's Silk, Feel It" and "Bop-A-Bye Lullabye."

I kept The Purple Onion (Los Angeles) open nearly two years before it closed.

There was a preacher who visited the prisons. From time to time, I would go along with him to sing. I still have a painting that one of the prisoners had given to me. Palm Springs, California was a very popular getaway at the time, and they always had entertainment. I used to go there to sing.

The Ye Little Club opened in Beverly Hills, California, and they hired me to perform. It became my standard ground base place. That is where I met a lot of the big-name entertainers. I had already met Sammy Davis Jr., and I have a photograph of us, but most of the people were White. One I will always remember was Rosemary Clooney, who was a singer and actress. Her song, "Come On-a My House," made her popular in the 1950s, and she was also one of the stars of the film, *White Christmas*. She told me if I ever got a chance to record, to be sure not to go with RCA Victor. I guessed she would know.

Later on, I met a country-western singer named Dorothy Shay. They called her the "Park Avenue Hillbilly." She had a series of hits on Columbia Records in the late 1940s, and appeared in a few movies, too. At the time I had met her, Dorothy wore fine gowns and worked in the big nightclubs, like Lena Horne. She had just finished singing at the Coconut Grove when she came into the club and saw me perform. One night, she told me she was going to take me on as her protégé. I didn't know what she meant and she explained it meant she was going to help me with my career.

"Why do you call yourself Frierson?" Dorothy asked.

"Because that is my real name."

"It is not a good name for show business."

"Why?"

"It is too long. I suggest you change the last name by making it shorter."

She thought for a while and suggested using Lester as my last name. That's how my show business name became Ketty Lester. I thought it was an easy name, so I went home and told Frank and Earn. Earn said, "That's a nice name," but Frank told me, "You will still be Re-V to me."

One day when I returned from a trip, Dorothy called to tell me she was taking me to the Coconut Grove to see Lena Horne perform. Miss Horne, who got her start as a chorus girl at the Cotton Club, was one of the most famous Black female performers of her time, still known to this day for her hit, "Stormy Weather." She was considered a great beauty, and starred in films, in nightclubs, and on Broadway. Dorothy introduced me to Lena and told her what she was trying to do for me. Lena came to see me after she closed at the Coconut Grove.

Dorothy told me she wanted to take me to New York for an audition. When I came home, I told Frank and Earn. They thought

Dorothy Shay, country-western singer and character actress. She was known as the "Park Avenue Hillbilly."

it was okay. The next day, Maya and I were together and I told her. Maya said, "No." I didn't understand why she would say no. I went on to explain that I had never been to New York and it wasn't costing me anything to go. She said, "No" again because she loved me. I didn't think that should have had anything to do with it and if she really loved me, why didn't she want to support me?

"It was not what you said, Maya, it's the way you said it."

I told her I loved her like a big sister and friend. I told her the way she was acting, it seemed as if she didn't want me to be successful in my career.

Finally, Maya relented. "No, no, no, you're right and I'm wrong. I want you to go to New York with her."

I told her I would be gone for only a few days. I was not planning to stay in New York. I would call her to let her know how things went.

Frankly speaking, I thought it was nice of Dorothy, a country-western singer, to try to help me. No one else had offered and I loved the idea and wanted to see New York. I had heard of it, but I had never seen it. This was when Maya had started to write her poems and had started talking about a play. Strangely, she was not in Los Angeles when I got back. I guess she had gone back to San Francisco. I didn't see her for quite a while. I think she had started writing her first book.

Starting College and Turning Pro

Maya had come back to Los Angeles and called me. When she was here and writing her poems, I didn't understand them at first. I liked poems that rhymed. After Martin Luther King, Jr., started fighting for voting rights for Black people, I understood them better. At the time, I didn't know people couldn't vote because my father had voted all his life. I didn't really know what was going on. Maya had started writing her book, *I Know Why the Caged Bird Sings,* but I never read it and I never saw the movie. Maya went on to form a great friendship with Oprah Winfrey. I wouldn't see her again until years later.

PART THREE
First Recording and First Boyfriend

Dorothy Shay and I flew to New York. It was my first time going there and being on a plane. I had the window seat and she told me when the plane reached altitude, I should try to get some sleep as it would be a long trip. I didn't know anything about altitude, so I asked her what it was and how I would know when we reached it.

She laughed at me. "Don't worry about it. I will let you know when we reach the cruising stage."

We got to New York and I had never seen so many people, so many cars, and taxicabs. It didn't take us long to get to our hotel. New York was not pretty to me. It was busy, just too busy. The things I remember most were the park, the horses, and buggies you could take to ride around the city.

First Recording and First Boyfriend

The first place Dorothy took me was that big old record company that Rosemary Clooney told me not to ever sign with—RCA Victor. I did the audition and they told her I didn't have a recording voice. Dorothy told me not to worry about them. Well, I didn't because if they had said yes, I would have had to say no. We went to some other places and rode in the horse and buggy wagons. We went to Rockefeller Center. I didn't like the places where the people lived in the brownstones. They had no porches and no yards, just steps down to the street. We were there for two weeks before we headed back. I was so glad to be home.

Dorothy got me an audition for the re-opening of George and Ira Gershwin's *Porgy and Bess*. The play was in Beverly Hills, and I played the part of Bess. I received good reviews, and it was the first show under my new name: Ketty Lester. This was my first singing and acting role. Years later, I found out they had recorded some of the show songs.

Dorothy told me she was going to talk to her friend, Betty Corday, who was the creator and owner of the soap opera, *Days of Our Lives*. Some way, Dorothy and Mrs. Corday came to an agreement and created a family of Blacks on that show. I played the character Mrs. Grant, who had a husband and two kids: a boy and a girl. We were on the show for about six or eight months, and that daytime soap opera is still on. Mrs. Corday is dead, though. I think

The Grant Family on "Days of Our Lives."
R to L: Me, Tina Andrews, Michael Dwight Smith, Lawrence Cook.

Me and Tina Andrews.

First Recording and First Boyfriend

her son might own it now. When they took the Grants off *Days of Our Lives*, I went back to singing at Ye Little Club.

Dorothy had to go make appearances for herself. One night, a boy named Ed Cobb, a member of The Four Preps, came to the club to see me. The Four Preps were on Columbia Records. They had hits on the charts, mostly in the 1950s and 1960s, and they backed Ricky Nelson on his parents' TV show, *The Adventures of Ozzie and Harriet*. Now, Ed Cobb was both a producer and a songwriter, and he went on to write a whole lot of very famous songs, like "Dirty Water" and "Tainted Love."

For three nights, they came to see me. Finally, Ed Cobb asked if I would make some tapes or demos for him.

"I don't care," I said, "and what time do you want me?"

Ed said, "Next week, around two o'clock in the afternoon." He gave me the place and address. It was the engineer's house where he had a studio over his garage.

The engineer's name was Armin Steiner. I believe he and Ed were the producers. I found out much later that Armin was working at Fox Studios as an engineer where he had been for years. I never saw him again to this day. Years later, there was a big article in the paper about him.

When I got there, I asked what he wanted me to sing.

"Just do what you do at the club."

The first song we recorded was "I'm a Fool to Want You." Lincoln Mayorga played piano and Earl Palmer was on drums. They had a bassist and guitarist that I did not know. We kept taping songs, but I got tired and could not think of more songs. Lincoln had "Love Letters" on the piano. I said, "I don't really know that song, but play it and I will sing it."

He played it but it was so straight.

I asked, "Can't you put a little soul in that song?"

"What's that?"

"Gospel, man," I replied.

He didn't even know gospel. I just gave it to him with my voice and hands. Earl finally got the beat and rhythm on the drums. We did "Love Letters" and I left.

After being at Ye Little Club for a couple of weeks, I went to Oregon for a while. When I returned to Ye Little Club, I had gotten there a little early. Lincoln Mayorga came in smiling, saying, "Your record is number 32 in Boston."

"What record?" I asked. "I haven't made a record. I did some tapes for you guys."

"Have you seen Ed?"

"No, I have not seen Ed."

It was time for my show. So, I performed it. Later, Ed Cobb came in with a big smile on his face, too. I just looked at him.

First Recording and First Boyfriend

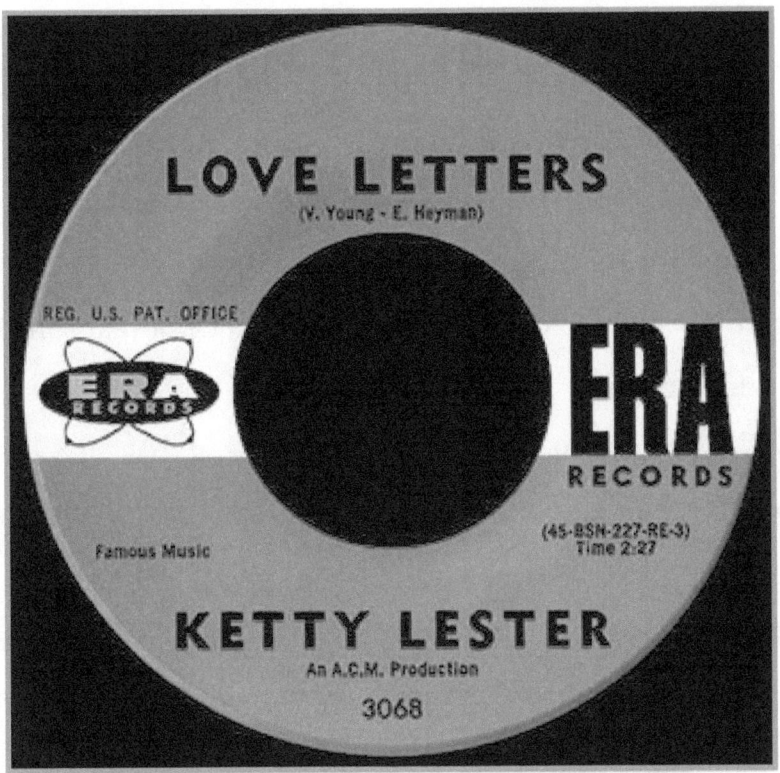

"Our demo has become a record and number 32 on the charts in Boston," he said. "That was not supposed to be a record, but the little record company wanted it."

"What company? What are you doing?"

"It was good, Ketty. The little record company wanted it, and I sold it to them."

"You are not my manager. What am I supposed to do? How could you do this to me?" I didn't know what else to say. He didn't even ask me. Dorothy wasn't there.

I started calling him stupid. I didn't know how to stop saying it. "I really didn't know "Love Letters." I only did it that one time on the demo for you guys. I don't even have sheet music for that song. I have no contract or agreement with you or that company."

Ed said, "It's Era Records."

"I have never heard of it, and how could they put that song out without talking to me or Dot?"

"Well, he wanted it right away and we let him have it."

I told him he had done wrong. "Well, I need to at least meet him."

Okay, they didn't even introduce me to the man. Lincoln wrote out the arrangement of the song for me, and he would go with me from time to time as my pianist.

So, I started singing it, but I never signed with Era Records. They once sent me a check for $3,200, but I got no more and I never met the owner, Herb Newman.

I had to go to New York, again. Since I had been there before and had seen how the people dressed, I decided to make me a new pair of slacks. I made them out of mohair, like the material once used for men's suits. I made them with wide bottoms. On the outside seam and middle seam, I put triangle pieces. On the bottom, they were different and were kind of nice because no woman had ever had pants made of mohair before.

First Recording and First Boyfriend

When I walked on Broadway, the women turned their heads, looking at me.

"Dorothy, why are they looking at me so?"

"It's your pants. They are different."

Well, I figured if they were that noticeable, I wanted a jumpsuit made of satin with wide bottom legs, because I was going to open at a jazz club in Greenwich Village called The Village Vanguard. At first, this club was a little like The Hungry Eye; it had mostly folk acts and poetry readings, but in 1957, it became a jazz club and since then, has featured some of the most famous jazz artists in the world. To this day, it's the oldest operating jazz club in New York City.

"Oh," Dorothy said, "I know someone who could make them for you."

She took me to one of her designers and had them make the jumpsuit for me.

"Well, they are cute," Dorothy remarked, "but just wear them some time for show."

She had given me a beautiful gown, but I thought since they were looking at my slacks so much, I should wear my body suit with the wide bottoms. They would even be better, so we did it opening night. The news was there, even that paper, *The New York Times*. My show went well. "Love Letters" was in the top 20 by then and climbing. "I'm a Fool to Want You" was on the jazz stations. My show was good, I got good reviews. *The New York Times'* reporter said I had a great voice, but I could have left those satin, bell-bottom overalls at home. Since he made fun of my pants, I kept his review. It was funny to me, but I wore my gowns from time to time, too. I only had about three gowns at the time.

About six months later, *Vogue* magazine debuted the first pair of bell-bottom pants on its cover and inside they had the bell-bottom blue jeans. They became big for years. Too bad I didn't have the designer rights from that bell-bottom pattern, but I did get that old newspaperman back. I sent him the front of *Vogue* and a note, "*What the hell do you think of the overalls now, damn it?*" So, you see, ol' Ketty opened another door. I wore those wide bottom pants in 1962, and bell bottoms didn't become all the rage until 1964.

It was strange; I never saw Dorothy anymore. Since she had left me, I began to think about my pants I made when I went to New York the second time, and the designer she took me to, who made my body suit. I began to wonder if they took my pattern and he made the pants that made so much money since I never heard from her again. She might have taken advantage of old country Ketty also. She got her money, so did he.

The hit, "Love Letters," got me with the GAC agency. That was where I started getting regular jobs. I got my first agent and had to sign with AFTRA (American Federation of Television and Radio), the union for singers. I had to start paying union dues. I should have been getting checks from that recording company, but I didn't.

First Recording and First Boyfriend

Every time I called the union about that, they would say I needed a lawyer. They informed me they didn't handle that part. What were they handling? I paid my dues every month. I called them but could get no information. AFTRA made more money off me than SAG (Screen Actors Guild), the acting union I retired from.

My record was a worldwide hit. In London, it was number 1. It was a hit in Japan and in Australia. In fact, Japan asked me to come there because it was a hit. I feared to go. I didn't speak the language, but should have known they would have taken care of me since they had asked me to come. Australia asked me to come, but I was by myself and was scared. I should have known they would have taken care of me because they asked me to come. I was just scared. I was in a big city by myself with nobody but the agent. I didn't know what to do. I wouldn't go anywhere unless I was going with someone. So here we are, alone with "Love Letters," still number 2. That record stayed on the charts around the world for a year and they continued selling it, but never paying me.

"Love Letters" had really changed things for me. I began to think it was because of that old war in Vietnam. People received letters from their families and tried to write back, not knowing if they would get it. People were in a desperate state of mind. Too many lives were lost during that war. A lot of Black men were sent over there. Later in the 1960s, then Senator, Robert F. Kennedy asked why all the Whites were in school and not fighting for their country, and Muhammad Ali went to jail because he protested the war and refused to join the service.

I learned I was going on thirty-two one-nighters with James Brown, of all people. I had never been in that kind of show and didn't think I would fit in with the other acts. I was to meet them in Georgia and do the first show. Then we would travel on a bus. The musicians and singers for the other acts, I didn't know. James Brown had his limo and was following the bus, I guess.

When we did the first show, they told me we should get something to eat and they showed me where the bus was.

It was the first time I'd seen James Brown. To me, he didn't sing that well, but he was a fine showman. I was on the bus and trying to sleep. My bus associates started to drink and smoke pot. Well, I never drank nor smoked and it smelled bad to me. I didn't have a blanket or sheet to cover up. I asked them if they could do that when we stopped, especially the pot. They laughed and smoked more.

I went to the bus driver and asked him to stop the bus. I got off and told him to go on. I was in the woods beside the road, thumbing a ride. When I saw a car, it just happened to be James Brown. Thanks to God, he stopped and asked me what I was doing out there. I said I got off the bus. He told me to get in and asked what happened. I told him I didn't drink and I definitely didn't use pot or drugs. I told him I would be leaving the show and going back

First Recording and First Boyfriend

to New York. I thanked him for the ride when we got to where I could get a plane. He paid me for the two days I'd worked. Maybe I lost out on a lot of opportunities because I did not drink, smoke, or do drugs of any kind. It was early in my career, and at that time, it was common knowledge that women were forced to do all kinds of things to get hired. I stuck to my guns, kept my faith, and just carried on the only way I knew how, waiting to see where God would take me.

I caught the plane and made it home to New York, to the YWCA where Dorothy had told me to live. I called my agent and told him the story and why I left. They said they understood and booked me at the Apollo Theatre. Dorothy had left me—why I don't know. I guess she did not understand the places where the agent was booking me. As my manager, it was her job to talk to the agents about that. Instead, she left. At the Apollo, they told me, "If you are not belting your head off or dancing your drawers off, they will boo you off that stage." I didn't know what I was going to do. That place was a shake, rattle, and roll performing place. Well, well, well. What the hell was I going to do? A soft singer with a lot of shake, rattle, and rollers.

It was opening night. I put on the finest, shining gown I had. It was the beaded gown Dorothy had given me. They hadn't seen one as sparkly as that. When I walked onto the stage, I held up one finger and walked to the microphone.

"Just one love letter," I said. They laughed and applauded. I sang it; they applauded me again. After two weeks of performing, I walked off that stage and that was that.

Someone to Write Love Letters To

A few weeks later, I joined Cab Calloway. Some of the acts who were going with Cab Calloway met. We were going with him to Italy. Now, you probably know that Cab Calloway was a famous big band leader from the 1930s, but did you know that he was the first Black artist to earn $1,000,000 from a single song? That's right, "Minnie The Moocher" was the song. Cab was also the first Black to have his own nationally syndicated radio program. It was through working with Cab that I met Audrey June Taylor and her dance act. After we met and took pictures, June asked if I wanted to go with her to a bar in Harlem. I told her I didn't drink. She assured me it was all right because she knew the bar and others in the show were going, too. It was the first time I had been in "just a bar" where you ordered a drink and had no entertainment. I ordered a 7-Up, and a young White man behind the counter asked my name. I thought he was going to say something about my having just a soda at the bar, so I said, "None of your business." Everyone started laughing. I was just sitting at the bar with June.

First Recording and First Boyfriend

Cab Calloway and me, with two other performers.

He asked if I would like to know his name. I looked at June and said, "Did I ask him for his name?"

Everyone started laughing at me again.

"Her name is Ketty," June told him.

"Girl, you don't have to talk for me."

He told me his name was Carlo Bilotti.

"That's nice," I said.

Then he said, "You're cute."

"Listen, I'm not cute."

"Then you are pretty."

I have never considered myself a pretty woman and thought he was making fun of me. So, I said, in a disgusted way, "You're nuts. Do you know that?"

I told June I was going to my room to get some rest and would meet her at the airport. I had to pack my bags.

He asked, "Where are you going?"

"I'm not telling you because you can't go anyway," I told him, and then said goodbye to June and took a cab to my room at the YWCA.

I met everyone at the airport and we embarked on our trip to Italy. It felt like the longest trip I'd ever taken. We got to Italy and who do you think met us there? You would never guess. Carlo Bilotti, the barman, of all people! It had to be June who told him where we were going and when we were leaving.

Everyone started laughing, and chanting, "Ketty's got a boyfriend."

Naturally, I told them to stop it. I didn't have a boyfriend because, basically, I was a loner. I didn't know anything about boyfriends.

"I don't know anything about this boy, so just stop it," I told them all.

I think he thought I felt bad or something. He explained he was from Italy and could help where we were going. He asked where we were staying and I told him I didn't know. He found out where we were staying and took June and me there, where June and I shared

First Recording and First Boyfriend

a room. We visited different places and were in Italy for about two months. He was there with us for the whole two months, always taking us to dinner or someplace. At least, we saved money on the food bill. Come to think of it, I don't know who paid for the hotel. Cab Calloway, I guess.

When it was time for us to come home, everyone was deciding when and what time they would leave. The director, Mervin Nelson, had found out about a new ship that was making its maiden voyage to New York. I'd never been on one so I told Carlo and June that I would be going back on the ship with the director. I felt safe because folks told me Mervin was gay, and he has always been nice to me. Carlo said it would be a long trip and he would see us back in New York.

It *was* a long trip. We had food and music all the time. People were dancing. I got so tired because that music seemed to be playing all night. I finally went to my sleeper.

The next morning, Mervin knocked on my door. He said he had been trying to get me up last night because there had been a storm and I could have drowned. I told him, "What you don't know can't hurt you." I had been asleep and it was time now for breakfast.

"Let's go get it."

It was time for us to be getting closer to New York and I was so glad. We had been on that ship for about two weeks. The sun was shining and I was so glad we would be docking soon.

Carlo Bilotti.

Carlo and me at the beach.

First Recording and First Boyfriend

Mervin and I were walking off the ship and someone said, "Hi, Ketty."

I looked up and who do you think was there? Carlo Bilotti.

"What is he doing here?" I asked.

I was glad to see him, though. I told him that Mervin was here, too. He asked where he lived. He drove Mervin to his house. This was the first time I had been alone with him. We went to a little restaurant on 54th Street and I had my 7-Up, as usual. We were there for about an hour, discussing the trip.

"How did you like the boat ride?" he asked.

"It was long, boring, and too much music. Lots of music and food all the time. If they wanted to, a person could eat twenty-four hours a day. There were stores to go shopping, but everything was so darn high, I could not buy anything."

Carlo felt he should have been with me to buy me anything I wanted.

"I didn't want anything."

"I told you that it would be a long trip," Carlo said. Then he changed the subject. "What are you doing tomorrow?"

"I have to talk to my agent."

I lived at the YWCA, a religious place where girls could get a room and live safe, because they did not allow men, not even for a visit. He was surprised he could not come in but got a phone number to call.

The next day, I found out I had an appointment with RCA Victor Records, of all people. I got there around 11:00 a.m. I told them right off that I did not want to be with them. They told me I didn't have a choice. They had bought my contract.

I didn't have a contract with them. He said it didn't matter, they had bought Era Records, and I had to sign their contract. I never heard from Ed Cobb, but Lincoln Mayorga worked with me from time to time and wrote my arrangements. I had not seen Dorothy Shay in a long time. She had left me, so it was me and RCA. That company had been just like Rosemary Clooney said. They could make or break you. I knew it was over for me after the first recording session with them.

They had an eighteen-piece band. I always liked singing with a small group and told them I could not sing over all those musicians.

They said, "Yes, you can. Just belt."

Well, here they go, trying to ruin a singer's voice. "Damn it." I did it and I kept singing pop songs. They never wrote new songs for me.

It seems like Carlo and I were always together after I got back. Sometimes, his brother and June were with us, but most of the time, it was just the two of us. When I had something to do, he would call to see how long I would be gone. Sometimes, he would take me. If I had nothing to do, he would pick me up and we would be alone together until we went to dinner.

First Recording and First Boyfriend

One day, he called and asked if I had eaten breakfast. I hadn't and Carlo told me to meet him in the lobby in half an hour.

While eating breakfast, Carlo started pouring out his heart and soul to me.

"I like you so much," Carlo said.

"Well, I like you, too."

"I really care for you. Do you trust me by now?"

"Yes, but I am a girl alone in a big city."

"I know, but from now on, you will not be alone. It will be you and me."

I didn't understand exactly what he meant, but we spent the day talking and going places. It was getting late and, as usual, he took me to dinner. Then he took me back to the YWCA. He told me to pack all my things and he would come for me. I asked him to let me think about it. Frankly speaking, I was at a loss to know what to think, because no boy had ever said anything like that to me. He put his arms around me. Normally, I would have started to fight—that was my nature—but not this time. For some reason, I liked him.

Three days later, he called and asked if I had packed my things. Of course, I had packed.

He said, "I'm moving you out of this place. I have an apartment and I'm moving you in." He paid the bill and we left.

The night that he took me away from the YWCA, he brought me to what I thought was 'my' apartment. I did not know that Carlo had other ideas. We sat on the couch and talked for a long time. Finally, Carlo said, "It's getting late. I guess it's time for bed."

Well, I know *I* thought so, but I was wondering when he was going to go home so I could go to bed.

"I'll go to bed as soon as you go home," I told him.

Now, he thought that was so funny. "I *am* home," he said. "I live here too. I'm here with you."

I looked around, and all I saw was one bedroom. "Well, where are you going to sleep? On the couch?"

"No," he said, looking toward that bedroom with the big round bed, "I'm going to sleep right there with you."

From then on, Carlo and I started living together, just the two of us in a world of our own, all by ourselves. We came from such different worlds, and here we were, making our own world together, one hidden away from everyone and everything, because that's the way it had to be in those days. But it really was like living in my own personal fairy tale with my own personal Prince Charming. Carlo promised me that he would protect me, and I guess he always did.

He was taking care of me. He would go to work at the bar and when I was not working, I stayed home until he came to get me to go to a show or someplace. He took such good care of me and I know he cared for me. We never asked each other a lot about our lives, we were just happy and it was a good time. We enjoyed life.

First Recording and First Boyfriend

A lot of people don't know how to enjoy life, but we did and were so happy. For me, he was the first man in my life.

We spent lots of time looking at art. He and his brother ran their bar. Sometimes, I would go with him or stay at home, unless I had an appointment. Carlo was always taking care of me. When I went off to sing, he took me to the airport and picked me up when I got back. I was still making records, too, for RCA.

Carlo would take me to fancy restaurants. He got something special to try before dinner. He asked me to taste it and I asked what it was. He told me it was escargot, which is what the French call snails.

"Now wait, I don't eat those things. They grow in the flowers and we kill those things. You can eat it, but I'm not."

He thought it was funny and asked what I wanted to eat. I told him I didn't know and he ordered me lobster. It was good. There were lots of "first time things" with Carlo.

I told him I wanted to see my family. It had been a long time. He said, "Okay. We'll go together to LA."

I called my agent before we left. The office said it was okay, but I had to be back in two weeks.

Carlo came with me and stayed at The Wilshire Grand Hotel downtown. I stayed with Earn and Frank. I went to the hotel during the day when they were at work. When it was about time for us to get back to New York, Carlo wanted to meet my family and told me to bring them to dinner. They agreed and we met at the restaurant in the hotel and had a good dinner. Frank was his usual joking self. Carlo told me later that Frank was more like me. Frank asked if Carlo was my agent and I told him he was a friend. I just didn't tell him he was my *personal* friend.

What you may not know is that interracial dating was illegal in some states in the 1950s and 1960s. We're not even talking about marriage…there used to be a set of laws called anti-miscegenation laws that were part of legal segregation. It meant you could go to jail for marrying someone of another race. In some places, if a mixed couple was seen in public together, they would fear for their lives. It wasn't until, thanks to Dr. King and the Civil Rights Act of 1964, that the anti-miscegenation laws disappeared, but it took until 1967 for the ban against interracial marriage to disappear all across the country. That was too late for Carlo and me.

When I returned from California, I found out I would be heading to England with the Everly Brothers, doing some one-nighters. Lincoln Mayorga went with me. It was for about a month. Phil Everly, the older one, played the guitar with us. The English were the best audience I ever had. I enjoyed being there, but it was over and I was back with Carlo. We would go to the beach, of all places. I couldn't swim. It was nice and he loved the beach.

By way of an invite, I went to Canada, a place I had never been. Carlo asked if I wanted him to go with me and I said, "No." It was

First Recording and First Boyfriend

just to Toronto. He asked when I was supposed to be there and for how long. I told him three weeks and he felt that it was a long time. He told me he would miss me so much. I told him I would miss him, too. "I am a singer and I have a record still on the charts. I enjoy playing clubs because at least you are in one place."

Carlo took me to the airport and, as always, went to the gate with me.

"I'll see you when you get back."

He would always give me a kiss on the forehead. Within three weeks, I was back and we were together again.

After two months, they invited me back to England. This time, I was by myself at The Cavern Club where The Beatles played. Now, you may ask why a singer like me would be playing in a rock and roll club. Well, in those days, most places were still jazz clubs and most young people went to places called milk bars and coffee bars. The Cavern was a jazz club at first, and only served soft drinks and coffee. When the Beatles started playing there, it was still mostly a place to hear jazz, and they didn't serve alcohol. The Beatles used to play there twice a day, and they would have to go down the street to a pub called The Grapes if they wanted to have a beer. It was a few years before The Cavern before stopped booking jazz acts and changed to a rock and roll only club.

I wanted to see Buckingham Palace in London. I had heard of that place ever since I'd been going to England. I wanted to see it. There was a gentleman who would take me there. I was a little shocked because the Palace was a big white building, with a driveway, and a fence and a gate made of wrought iron. The driving space inside was dirt.

I just asked, "What kind of car does she ride in?"

"A beautiful wagon," the gentleman said.

"Do you know I have been riding in wagons all my life on dirt roads?"

"Does the wagon have a motor?"

"No, it is pulled by big horses."

"Horses? My brother Ezekiel's horse, Bugger Red didn't pull no wagon."

I had never seen the Wells Fargo horses. "Are you sure those are not mules?"

"Oh no, these are special horses."

I did not know the wagon was an antique.

"Where does the Queen get all of her money?"

"From the people."

"Oh, you pay your taxes to the Queen? Those uniforms need to be cleaned and pressed. After all, they are working for the Queen. She does pay, doesn't she?" We both had a good laugh.

"Okay, Ketty."

I looked up at the top of the building and it looked as if the paint was coming off. Again, I made a fool of myself. "Do you know

First Recording and First Boyfriend

this palace needs painting? Look up there, the paint is coming off!"

"Come on, Ketty, let's go."

"Okay, okay."

But I know what I saw and what I said was true. "Did I insult the Queen?"

"You insulted everyone."

"Oh, no. I'm so sorry."

"Don't worry about it. Just sing for the people like you do."

"I'll do my damnedest."

"Let's get you some food. You rest and I'll pick you up later." He laughed.

I'd done something stupid, as usual. Something else I realized about London was that they had the driest damn sandwiches of any place I'd ever been.

So, again, here I go. "Don't they have lettuce, tomato, mayonnaise?"

He took my sandwich back and got the condiments added, whatever it was.

"Have you ever been to America?" I asked. I would take him to get some real food. Raised on a farm, I loved vegetables.

We had the best time that night with the people of England. I was there for about a week or two and had a packed house every show. People lined up every night to see me. Today, I say with a grateful heart, England was my greatest audience.

It was good to see Carlo when I got home and I was not ashamed to say it. We went to dinner and he tried to trick me with some chocolate ants.

"Not me," I said, "I don't eat that. I'll just have a steak."

After a couple of weeks of messing around, I managed to get an off-Broadway show. It was a reopening of "A Cabin in The Sky." It ran for quite a while. I was lucky to get good reviews and won the off-Broadway Award. They called it the Theater World Award. Each year, I still receive an invitation to attend the presentation.

Carlo took me to the dinner place again and asked if I had ever heard of caviar. I had heard of it but never tasted it. He ordered me some. I tasted it, but it was raw and I don't eat raw fish guts. He cracked up and said it wasn't fish guts, but eggs.

"I don't eat raw chicken eggs." And I had not until he took me to the restaurant and ordered me Eggs Benedict for breakfast.

He ordered me lobster as before. Then we went home to rest and talk.

"I want to take you somewhere special," Carlo said.

Naturally, I said, "Where?"

"It is a surprise trip. When will you have some time off?"

"I think in about two weeks."

"Tell your agent you'll be away for a couple of weeks, okay?"

Well, the time was just about to come and we were getting ready to start packing for our trip. In a few days, we were ready to leave.

First Recording and First Boyfriend

We get on the plane, first class. We're on our way. They used to serve dinner on planes. We had dinner and settled back. I went to sleep in his arms and stayed that way for a few hours. When I woke up, I asked him where he was taking me.

"To meet my mother," Carlo said.

I was a little shocked, so I asked, "Do you think that's a good idea?" Knowing what I know about people, I was thinking he was a little shy about life or race, even his own, but I settled back. Coming from Arkansas, knowing all I know about White people and how Black people have had to suffer, it was only natural for me to be concerned. As long as it was the two of us I was okay, but with his mother then I was a little fearful.

You would be, too, coming from the country and going to a foreign country, not speaking the language. I wouldn't know what they were saying. I was lost. In my past world, we didn't know about nationalities, we only knew either White or Black. They told me my grandmother was part Indian, but I had never seen one.

We finally made it to Rome, got our hotel, and went out walking. I really didn't know what to say and kept wondering what had I gotten myself into.

It was the day we were going to see his mother. He had bought me a new dress and told me his mother was Baroness Miceli. She was born into the royal Italian family. I didn't know what to say, think or do. I was supposed to meet this woman with her son. *She'll kill me*, I thought. *She'll have me killed.* Italy is known for its Mafia, not royalty. I was not saying anything. We were going to Milano. That's where she lives.

"How far is it from here?"

"Not too far." He put his arm around me. "You're acting afraid. You don't have to be. You are with me. Everything will be just fine."

I knew he cared about me but knowing life as I did, it was a natural feeling I had—I think.

When we got there, he hugged his mother and introduced us. I just said in English, "It's nice meeting you." I had forgotten her name except for Baroness. We stayed there for the day and had dinner with her. They talked in their language. She was a pleasant woman and I tried to be the same. When we left, she said, "It was nice to have met you." Carlo hugged her and looked at her funny.

If she was trying to hurt me, she didn't. The one she really hurt was Carlo. We stayed for the rest of the time. He took me to Venice. It was an interesting place, surrounded by water. We had to take a boat to get there. I didn't get off the boat. He told me his family had an art gallery there. He wanted me to see the gallery, but I was still a little confused after meeting his mother. I never found out what she thought of me.

Finally, it was time to go home. He was nice and sweet to me, but when we got back, he became a little pushy for me to have a child. I just said, "I don't think I can have children."

Carlo responded, "I am going to send you to the best research center in the country."

He decided to send me to the Margaret Sanger Research Center. I didn't know anything about that place, but I did know how to protect myself. There was an old woman back in Beverly Hills who told me how to do that and I never forgot it.

Carlo was my first male friend, and I was a virgin. I never just lay in bed after sex. I got up right away and cleaned myself off. I always remembered what that old woman had said. My mother always said, "No license, no babies," so, it wasn't going to happen to me. After about three months, I did not think I was learning anything at Margaret Sanger, and not planning to marry. He never talked about marriage.

One night, we were talking and I asked him, "Why is having a baby so important to you?"

We had been together for a long time and enjoyed each other's company. "You've taught me about male life," I said.

"I just want a child with you," Carlo said.

A child and no marriage, I thought. *No, you're putting it all on me.*

I told him my mother had fifteen kids and I had no doubt about my being able to have children. It's just a matter of when.

"How do you know it's not you?" I asked.

I think he was hurt and disappointed. We had never had a disagreement or fuss, but that's life. This was something special.

After a few months, he came home and said this was the last night we would be together. I had begun to expect that. I said fine and started packing all my clothing. I got them packed and asked him for four pieces of art. He was just sitting there.

"You can have whatever you want."

Next, I called and made my flight arrangements. He said he would have the artwork packed and mailed to me. I had to trust him and he did keep his word. The next morning, I told him I would need to go by my agent's office to let them know I would be moving to Los Angeles, and give them the information. They had a part of their office there. They gave me the number and the name of the man I was to call.

We had almost a day. We went back to the apartment, got the paintings, went to the post office, got a packing box, packed and mailed them. We had our last dinner. I was hurt, so there wasn't much to say. I think he was a little hurt, too, but it was his idea. So that was that.

Well, it was time for me to go to the airport. When we got there, he asked if I wanted him to go to the gate with me. I told him I can make it by myself. After about an hour, it was time for me to get on the plane. I was at the gate, boarded the plane and hours later, I decided to write my goodbye poem.

First Recording and First Boyfriend

So, I'll leave New York City today
I'm a little lonely, but I'm on my way
Another time of great love and joy, now tears
With someone who I felt really cared
It's been a beautiful time, the two of us together
But it's over now. It couldn't have been better
On the plane, I think of the good times we had.
Oh, yes, I think. But we must forget the past
I'll just think about tomorrow, tomorrow, tomorrow
I start to laugh, but then it turns into sorrow
I may find someone else as days go by
We may love each other in a deeper way than you and I
It's a long journey this day from New York to LA
I think I will try to sleep for a while, but first I'll pray
Goodbye, my friend, it's been a beautiful time
I hope you'll enjoy the rest of your life as I intend
to do with mine.

I really didn't want to leave New York because I had learned to love it, and I loved him. When I asked Carlo why he loved me, he always said, "You are so beautiful to me, I just love you."

He was the only person I knew there, except for my agent. I didn't know where June was, so I decided my best bet was to come home. I guess in a sense, it turned out better for me because I had already been on television, acting. When I got to Los Angeles, I made a commercial and that continued my career as an actress.

As time went on, my acting career got to be a little stronger, especially with Dr. King fighting for roles for the average Black woman. They gave me a few more commercials to try to shut him up. They couldn't shut him up until he was gone. Yes, I had the ability, but I thank him for my continued success in acting. It was his work, not mine, but they used old Ketty again.

First Recording and First Boyfriend

Commercials for:
Miracle 409 (top); Wesson Oil (bottom)

PART FOUR

My Two Big Mistakes and Marriage, Motherhood, Movies, and TV

Family Values

I made it back home to Los Angeles and my family. I was so glad to see my mother, my father and older sister, Clem. All were in Los Angeles with us. Frank had opened a lock and key shop and was doing fine.

Earnestine was still at Douglas Aircraft and had been there for quite a while. She had a friend who was an engineer and they were getting married.

It was so good to be home. I had been away for close to three years. We were going to church like old times. I even sang in the choir with Frank. I had not done that in years and to be with my own people was great, too. I met new people at church. One girl was as crazy as I was. She was fun and her name was Erma Tolliver.

After Carlo and I separated, it was a very desperate and lonely time for me. I didn't do anything except go for long walks and cry.

My Two Big Mistakes, and Marriage, Motherhood, Movies, and TV

Of course, I would do the cooking for the house, but it was like learning how to cook all over again. I had not cooked for years because I was eating out all the time. The food served in restaurants was not soul food. I had to learn how soul food was prepared all over again. Mama was there to help; if I forgot, I would just ask her. Living with Mama, I soon became a good cook again.

I used to help Mama quilt, but when I got back, she had quit quilting. She was crocheting and I tried to learn to do that, but mine would get too tight and I would have to unravel it. I found some art places and started buying paintings as we did in New York, but the paintings I got from Carlo are still my favorites. Besides going to art stores, I also started going to antique shops. I would go there just to try to keep myself busy and not think about the past. It was such a hard time for me and I never really got over Carlo. I simply accepted it.

One day my mother saw or heard me crying after I came into the room where she was and asked me what was wrong. Naturally, I said, "Nothing."

She wanted to know why I was crying if nothing was wrong. I told her I was not working enough and I was just a little worried. She told me not to worry, just pray and God would work things out for me. She asked if I wanted her to do the cooking. I told her no, that I had decided what to cook and I had it out, ready to prepare.

I'm always thinking of the future and what might happen. One day, there was a knock at the door. It was a man from Forest Lawn selling graves. I told my sister, Clem, "We should buy two of them—one for Mama and Papa and one for me and you." We didn't ask Mama and Papa, we just bought them.

I thank God for my family and the values that they gave me. I have tried to always be there for them, and during this tough time after I left New York and Carlo, they were there for me. Even though we were in Los Angeles, and not Arkansas, I felt as though I went back to my roots, cooking soul food with Mama, baking all her delicious cakes, quilting, and going to church together. But, no matter how broke my heart was, and no matter how safe I felt with them, I knew I still had a career to think about

I was a nightclub singer, but there weren't many nightclubs in the mid 1960s. Rock and roll had taken over. It was a matter of what I would do. If I did not do one-nighters, I would be out in the cold. The agent called and said there was a commercial for me. I had been home for almost a year before I started making commercials. I had made several, but now I'm having to read for them, like a show. When you're hurting, it's always good to keep yourself busy.

First, I would go to church and then Clem, Mama, and I started going to Bible study. I believe Mama always knew there was something bothering me, but she never pushed me or ever asked me about my past life. In those days, it seemed time was slow to pass.

My Two Big Mistakes, and Marriage, Motherhood, Movies, and TV

It seemed as if I always had to be the one to give and never get, but that, too, was a part of life and learning.

I spent some time with the people who were with Dr. Martin Luther King, Jr., in Georgia, where he got the voting rights bill passed. He then started fighting the movie industry for the ordinary Black woman, not just the light-skinned people or the fat women as maids. That's when they started using me in those commercials. They considered me an average Black. I never knew how much they paid the White people, but they only paid me $500.00 for the filming of one. You made your money when the commercial aired. They only aired mine three or four times. That way, I was only getting $500.00 minus 10% to the agent. Then the reruns were $35.00 per run and the agent got 10% of that. So, they were using old Ketty again. Dr. King and the bus riders walked through those doors for equality and voting and I would walk through those doors of show business.

I went to Brazil for a while with some man who entertained the soldiers. That was another long trip. I said to myself, *I'll never make that trip again.* With the traveling and the entertainment, we were gone for about three or four weeks or more. I don't remember, but it was an interesting trip. They had lots of jewelry and I bought myself two different rings—one with a yellow stone and one with a black pearl, which was supposed to be rare. We made it back and I was glad to be home with my new friends and my family.

I received a letter from Carlo, which was a surprise. The letter was nice and he said he missed me so much. Well, I missed him, too. He asked me to come back to New York so we could try all over again. I didn't answer the letter because I felt there was no future for us as a couple. I was a Black countrywoman and he was a White Italian. In those days, the rule was to stay with your own kind. I never thought that things would change, and that interracial marriage would ever be legal. I couldn't even imagine a time when couples like Carlo and me wouldn't have to hide or lie about our relationship. Those days were coming, but they weren't here yet, so I decided to let Carlo go. That was my first big mistake.

I didn't know if I would ever find a Black man that would accept me as I was because I was very outspoken and tough. If someone said something that was wrong, I would tell them what I thought, felt, and believed. I had always been that way and I have not changed in my older years. I can also say I'm sorry and ask for forgiveness. That was the way my parents raised me, and that is what the Bible says. So be it.

I got another one of those cheap commercials. I don't remember what it was, but it was the same cheap deal.

I had been home for about two years and I received an offer to go to Boston. I had never been to this club before so we would see how they liked old Ketty. The time had passed and it was opening night. As always, the press was there. The next day, I would know what they had to say about me. I did my show and I think I was all right. It was a little torchier than usual, but I think it was okay, under the circumstances.

Well! I got a really great review in the newspaper. It was *The Boston Globe*. Now, how about that? I read it. Oh, my! I think that the reporter really liked me. I think I'll keep it. I believe that old *Boston* reporter enjoyed my singing. He had put me in the class with Sarah Vaughn, Dinah Washington, and Ella Fitzgerald, who were great jazz singers, but I couldn't scat, I just sang.

I visited the girls and Cot in San Francisco for a few days. They were fine. Mattie was married now. Berneice had married again and had a nice husband. Amanda and Frank, Jr., were fine and so was Cot.

In Los Angeles, Ms. Clem was doing assistant teaching and going to Cal State LA to get her teaching degree. She'd have it soon, knowing her.

Seems like everyone was all taken care of, except for Ketty. What was in store for me?

I made another commercial for Tide. It was the first time I knew about the product. Of course, I've never seen the commercial, but they did send the agent little checks.

When I was home it was good to do the cooking for Mama and Papa and to see them sitting and resting for a change. They had worked so hard for their children. I went to the key shop and

DR. CARLO FRANCO BILOTTI
360 EAST 65TH ST.
NEW YORK, N.Y., 10021

8-18-65

My dear Ketty,

how are you? Did you ever get married? In Italy every thing is fine and every body asked me about you. Do you know one thing? I still love you! Will you ever come

My Two Big Mistakes, and Marriage, Motherhood, Movies, and TV

here?

I'll have the exhibition of my collection in three museums in January, including Los Angeles. I may come there.

Let me hear from you — I love you

Barb

got Frank so he would be with us for supper before going to bed. It would be like old times again with "funny boy" making his jokes. Papa was getting a little old and sickly, but he was still fun, too.

I got another job offer in Las Vegas and would be performing in the entertainment bar. Back in those days, you had the main room where the big names would go, the medium bar with entertainment—that's where I was—and the small bar for drinking. I think that was the Sands Bar that I was in. I was there for about three or four weeks. I didn't like Las Vegas. It was just too busy and loud for me, but I made it. They had big hotels and I lived where I worked and I ate where I lived. I would also play the nickel machines but never won anything. One time I won $10 but no big money. When I got back home, I said I would never work there again, and I didn't.

One Last Love Letter and A Brand-New Love

Since being back, I had been several places and a lot of time had passed. The time I was home, except for the commercials, I spent with my mother and father, and laughing and talking with Frank. I got a gig to work at the Playboy Club. Lincoln Mayorga had gone back East, so I had to find a new pianist. He was nice and was Black. I worked in the upstairs entertainment room. There was a bar on the main floor. My pianist would go to that room sometimes after the show.

One night, he met two, well-dressed, Black men. He asked if they had ever heard of me. Naturally, they had not. He told them I was good and that he played for me upstairs and they should come to see me. Their names were Bill and Norman. Bill asked me to have a drink.

"I don't drink, but I'll take a 7 Up."

Bill came back a couple of times while I performed at the Playboy Club. Finally, he asked if he could come to see me. I said, "If you want to, but you must know that I live with my parents." We started seeing one another when we had time. We were both working at that time. He had two jobs: one was at the Veteran's Hospital, and the other was as a truck driver with Texaco Oil, the first Black man to do that.

One day, I asked if he was religious and he said he was born a Baptist.

"Do you go to church?" I asked.

"I'll go with you."

"Do you believe in God?"

"Yes."

"If you believe in Him, why don't you serve Him?"

After that, Bill started going to church with me on Sunday, having dinner with us and then going to work. Later, I would go to the club and do that for another two weeks.

The last week at my work, I told him he was trying to do too much and when I was not working, I would help him with that truck, if he wanted to teach me. I was a quick learner. I could make the last delivery at 3:00 p.m. I always wanted to learn how to drive those big trucks.

We made arrangements for me to be in the parking lot. I told him, "Blink your lights when you're coming out of the gate and I will get in the truck."

The truck had just about six gears up to cruising speed and six gears to hit the brakes to break it down to the stopping speed. I had learned it in about three nights and in a week I had it all. It also made me a better driver of any automobile, especially parking. Even today, I'm a pretty good parker. I learned how to drive that old red Texaco Oil tanker truck. It was interesting to me just to learn to do that. It also gave me something else to do.

So, Bill and I started dating. He was the first Black man I ever kept company with. I thought that it was strange that he and his friends never came to see my shows before. They did not know that I had records out. I didn't think many Blacks knew about the record. My brother, Frank was the only one in my family who had one. Now, this was something new for me. I would see how things would go as time went on. Well! He would have to wait and see. That also went for me.

Now he had started to ask me to marry him.

I said, "I'm not marrying anybody. Do you understand that?"

Here it came again. I said, "If you say that one more time, it's over. Do you hear me? Why should I marry someone I don't care about?"

One day, we were both off work together and he drove to the courthouse. "We're getting our license," Bill said.

"For what?"

"We're getting married."

"Are you joking?" I asked him because there was no love in this relationship for me. We were two friends who got along and worked well together.

So, we got the license, and he asked Frank to be the witness.

"When we get home," I said, "I'll tell Mama."

And that's what I did. "Do you know what you're doing?" Mama asked me.

I said, "No." I really didn't, but I was getting older and he was the only Black man I ever knew and he asked me to get married. I guess I'd better take the chance while I still had it. Do you know that I never dated another one of us in my life?

So, here we go. We were at the church.

"I have something to tell you," Bill said.

"What?"

"I have to pay child support."

"Have you been paying it?"

"No."

"Well, you are going to start, damn it, hell. We are at the church and you should have told me and this would not be happening."

We walked into the church and there was Frank, my niece, Deloris, and Reverend C.D. Toliver. We got married.

Well, that was my second and biggest mistake. I had made it and I would have to live with it or die trying. My parents didn't believe in divorce, so that was that. My next mistake was not going in with Hayward to buy an apartment building, taking one of the apartments and keeping my house for my mother and father. At that time, I could have done that. I loaned Ernestine about $7,000.00. I should have gotten the apartment for myself, lived in it and paid for my home and kept it.

The commercials kept coming in for me and that was good. I received another letter from Carlo. We had not seen nor talked to each other for three years. I found out he had gotten his doctorate degree and had opened three museums—one in New York, one in Rome, and one in Los Angeles. He would have probably come to Los Angeles if he'd heard from me. Well, I answered his letter, but never mailed it. He dated his later the 16th of August, but he didn't say Happy Birthday. (See Carlos's letter on pages 116-117.)

My letter to Carlo explained that I had just married a man I was not in love with and would never be in love with. I was honest with him. I told him we would be friends. I married him because

My Two Big Mistakes, and Marriage, Motherhood, Movies, and TV

he was my own kind and the only Black man who ever paid any attention to me. It was very odd that he would ask me to marry him. I couldn't really answer this letter because it would have hurt us both. Him, because he said he still loved me, and me, because I still loved him. Why write when it had to be something like this?

My dear Carlo.

I was married just two months ago, June 25th, 1966. Neither one of us was patient enough to wait for God to do His will. I hurt you because of what I said. You because of what you did. I still love you very much and always will. You were my first and only love and it will last forever.

I hope that you will find someone that you can forget about me and have the child that you so desperately wanted me to have and be happy. I should have stayed at Margaret Sanger like you wanted me to do. I do not blame you; I blame myself for our unhappiness. Please forgive me. This is hurting me to write just as it would hurt you to read.

I'll always love you.

I cannot mail this letter.

I never mailed that letter. I still wonder how different my life would have been if I made different choices. I wonder how things would have been if there was no racism. Would Carlo and I have gotten married? Would we have had the child he so desperately wanted? All I know is that I could not predict the future. I thought

I was doing the right thing even though it broke my heart. Carlo went on to marry someone else, too. I found out later that he had married in 1968. He did end up having a child, but she died of cancer at twenty years old. When I heard this, my heart broke for him, but I thought, what if we had had a child? Would he or she have died young, too? Well, what's done is done. I had made my decision. I said goodbye to Carlo, but I never mailed that letter. I didn't have the heart to, and I would never see him again.

Two New Arrivals—A Baby Boy and Epilepsy

My brother, Ezekiel's wife had left him. Until he found a place for him and his teenage son to live, I kept his son, Keith, my nephew. He attended Hamilton High School, which was close to me. One day, my nephew came home and told me one of his teachers had told the class that they didn't have to go to college to get a job.

I paused before answering. "That is true, but a teacher should not tell Afro-American boys they don't have to go to college. Some of them may not be able to, but you will be able if you want to go."

I didn't tell my nephew that I would be at school the next day. I just asked the name of the teacher and what time the class began.

Well, I went to the classroom, asked the teacher if he taught the class and how he became a high school teacher. He told me he went to college and majored in education. I told him I knew he had gone to college to become a teacher.

"You see that young man? That is my nephew, Keith, right there, who I am caring for at the moment.

"He said you told the class they didn't have to go to college to get a job. I don't know what you meant, but I don't like it and I don't think you should teach that again."

I embarrassed my nephew—not on purpose—and the other kids started laughing. I faced the class. "What I am saying is not to cause embarrassment nor is it a comedy routine."

I told them that is the past and now is the present. Education is very important and very necessary, especially for African-Americans. Education is better than sacrifice. You may say sacrifice your education, but in the long run, you may be sacrificing yourself.

"You see, experience and learning are better than sacrifice. The one thing my father told me as a child, and I have never forgotten is, 'You can learn something from a fool, but you must be intelligent enough to listen.'"

Then I addressed the teacher. "You are in the classroom to teach, educate, and, hopefully, encourage. That's what you are paid to do and I hope, from this day forward, that is what you will do. It was a pleasure to be here."

The teacher nodded. "Thank you so much, Ms. Frierson."

I turned around and left.

What I was trying to say, maybe not perfect, was to do and take advantage of all possibilities. It may be successful and it may be your last chance.

Well, time passes on, doesn't it? My first movie was *Uptight* in 1968, with Raymond St. Jacques, Frank Silvera and Ruby Dee. Now, did you know that Ruby Dee also wrote that screenplay? Imagine that, a Black woman writing a screenplay for a film, and starring in it, too. I played the part of Alma, and I got good reviews from it. Although I had the shortest part, it was a dramatic part. It was a Black revolutionary film, something about fighting for our rights. Nobody but me got reviews from the *Los Angeles Times,* and it was one of the first Black movies. The *Los Angeles Times* was giving reviews for all of the shows and it said something like, "Don't forget to give a soul cheer for Ketty Lester in *Uptight.* She did a great job."

My first movie role as "Alma" in Uptight, 1968.

My Two Big Mistakes, and Marriage, Motherhood, Movies, and TV

My brother, Hayward, worked all the time. He had three jobs, took care of his kids and his wife. She was sick, too, but every now and then, he would come to my house at about four or five o'clock in the morning and ring the bell.

Bill would say, "Who is ringing that bell at this time of the morning?"

I always knew it was Hayward. I would just say, "Stay in bed. I'll get it."

We would talk, have coffee and I would fix breakfast if he wanted it. He would bring me some kind of fruit he grew in his backyard.

When Hayward's son, David, finished high school, he received a scholarship to Cal Poly University in Pomona. He was a good runner. His father asked me to take him there and I did. That school was just starting its athletic department. Naturally, I would go to the school from time to time, to check on him. One day when I was not working, I went to see him run. He was good, but the team was not that good. He finished school and became the coach at Crenshaw High School. As usual, I went to a couple of his games when I had time.

It was 1972 and my next movie was coming up. This was the first Black horror movie, kind of a Black version of Dracula. Would you believe I was one of the stars? The movie was *Blacula* and I was known very well for that movie. I played the part of the taxi cab

Scenes from Blacua, 1972.

My Two Big Mistakes, and Marriage, Motherhood, Movies, and TV

driver bitten by Blacula. As a result, I became a vampire. To this day, people still talk about that film. I guess it became what you call a 'cult classic.' Isn't that something?

It was getting close to the holidays, Christmas and New Years. I felt a little tired, working and cooking. I had to do a lot of cooking because the whole family came for Christmas, including the grandchildren. Mama and Papa would spend Christmas Eve with me, so it was natural that the whole family would be there. My cousin, Malvin Forbes, would always be there, too. Ezekiel would buy the big twenty-four-pound turkey. I cooked everything, ham, greens, turnips, you name it, we had it. We had our special cornbread, and cornbread dressing for the turkey, and it was just like being back home.

I'd make all our childhood favorites for dessert, too. Mama's German chocolate cake with black walnuts instead of pecans in the frosting, and butter-roll would be on the table, just like back in Arkansas. It is a family recipe, and a family favorite. We loved to celebrate the holidays together, and Mama would arrange for family reunions, too. There'd always be a very busy kitchen on special occasions. In fact, every Christmas we would always have thirteen desserts. We'd have a chocolate coconut cake, two pound cakes, white cake, chocolate cake, yellow cake, fruit cake, two pecan pies, a lemon meringue pie, Momma Frierson's butter rolls, bread pudding, and tea cakes.

A week after that particular Christmas, on New Year's Day, I got sick.

"You're pregnant," Mama said.

Well, she should know. From that day on, I was vomiting and sick. I learned lots of women had that kind of pregnancy, during that time. They took a pill called Thalidomide sent from Germany and it damaged their babies. My doctor didn't give me anything and I was sick for the whole year. Someone told me to get some Chinese salt plums and I did. It helped me with the daily sickness you get from that condition. I kept working and singing, though. My doctor got cancer and had to retire. He turned me over to two young doctors. They were stupid.

I met them and realized they were not too smart. My old doctor had told me my baby's head was on my left side. When I started going to them, there was a knot in the middle of my stomach. They didn't think too much of it. I asked them about it and they told me it was my baby's head. I told them what Dr. Jones had said. He had said my baby's head was on my side.

"No, that is my baby's head."

I never gained but about ten pounds, but you could still see and feel the knot in my stomach. I was still singing and wearing my gowns at work. I had special gowns to wear. No one knew my condition. I do believe if the doctors were smart, they would have told me to take some calcium. It would have been helpful for me and the baby. I didn't think of it myself. This was another of my biggest mistakes, being careless with myself.

My last singing job was in August at the Apollo Casino in Atlantic City, New Jersey. I was there for two weeks. On the last night, the announcer called me out and asked, "Where are you going after tonight?"

"Back to Los Angeles to have a baby."

"Oh, oh, how many months are you?"

"Nine."

"And you haven't told us?"

"Have my shows been all right?"

Everyone laughed

"Oh, yes!"

"Then let me finish and get out of here." The audience and I had fun.

Just before I sang my last song I said, "This is me singing, not the baby" Ha!

I finished and left the next day. I made it home and, two weeks later, still no baby. If I ate or drank anything, I was still vomiting.

Earnestine and I went shopping. Earn bought a new dress to wear when we went to the hospital.

One day, I was in my yard asleep on the grass and Earnestine picked me up and took me to Mama's. I went to sleep on the bed.

When I got up, one drop of water hit my foot. I called Bill and he told me to go home and that we were going to the hospital. Earn took me home and she went to put on her new dress, but couldn't find it. She was so excited for me. I took a bath and got dressed. When Bill came home, I told him I was waiting for Earn. He called her and told her to come on and told me to get out of all that stuff I was wearing because I was going to the hospital, not a nightclub. Ha!

When we arrived at the hospital, I was still not having any pains or water breakage. The nurse gave me an enema and the pains started about five minutes apart. I would push and told the nurse to watch for the baby as I wanted a natural childbirth. I told her I would push and she would catch the baby. They called those crazy doctors and they told me not to push. How could you not push with those pains? They turned me over and shot me in the back. When they turned me back over, there was my baby. Crazy! They did not have to give me a shot, they did not ask me, and I didn't ask them for that.

William Kenneth Buckley is my child's name. He was named after his grandfather.

There was that knot still in my stomach that they had said was my baby's head. Three days after birth, the two doctors called and said it was a tumor and I would have to come back to the hospital

My Two Big Mistakes, and Marriage, Motherhood, Movies, and TV

My son, William Kenneth Buckley.

Mama holding my son, William.

My family: Bill, William, and me.

My husband, Bill.

Bill and William.

so they could remove it. They said it could be malignant and that word scared me. The doctors said it would take another three days. I asked if they would shoot me in the back again and they said they would see. I told them we should wait before surgery because they had given me a shot in the back three days before. They said, because of my condition, they had to remove the tumor. They would try to do their best. I said just put me to sleep and take it out. Naturally, doctors know best. Some of them are not as smart as they think. They did the surgery and that was another mistake, theirs not mine.

When I was supposed to go home, I got up and my head was drawn back to the spine. They gave me a shot and I had to lay on my back for three days. After the three days, I went home and no more drawing of the head, but that night I had my first grand mal seizure. Bill had asked me to have him a son. He got his son and I got seizures. They would occur at night. I took regular medication for epilepsy. I took them and continued working. Earn and Mama kept the baby and I prepared to do a commercial.

I thought I was getting better, so I went to Oregon to sing for two weeks. Earn kept the baby for me. She had two little boys of her own. I made the trip and before I knew it, I was back. Earn was waiting at the airport with my baby. Do you know he wouldn't come to me? *If I ever get his butt back, that will be the last time he does that to me*, I thought. I finally got him back. I called my agent and told him I didn't want to go out of town for long trips for a while. I would work in town.

While at the airport, Earn said, "I have something to tell you when we get home."

"Please tell me now," I encouraged her, holding my breath at the same time. What could it be?

She told me Bill was on his way from the VA Hospital to the Texaco Plant and the police found him in his car, with his first heart attack. They had taken him to Centinela Hospital. They didn't give him surgery, but he had to stay in the hospital for quite a while. Meanwhile, I was raising my son and caring for his father.

After Bill got out of the hospital, he started working for a real estate company. He was not doing that much, just helping himself have money, which he always saved for himself. I don't think he really believed that the first attack meant that he had a bad heart. He always wanted to eat what he wanted to eat, not what he was supposed to. Of course, he did not help me. He would just tell me when I had a seizure. It seemed that his heart problem was mine, too, but my epilepsy wasn't his. I guess that was my business.

I still believed that having the spinal shots, three weeks apart, once they delivered my baby and again when I had the surgeries to remove the tumors were the cause of my epilepsy.

The Magic of Black Television and Movies

As time went on, I took the role of Ruth in *A Raisin in the Sun* at the Ebony Showcase with Bea Richards and Paul Winston. I got good reviews.

My Two Big Mistakes, and Marriage, Motherhood, Movies, and TV

They finally started the first Black series on television called *Julia*, starring Diahann Carroll. The producer came to see *A Raisin in the Sun* and asked if I would like to make some guest appearances on *Julia*.

"Yes, when I finish this show," I said. I gave him my agent's number and name. It was no big thing to me. I had already been on a television show a few years ago, playing the role of Mrs. Grant on *Days of Our Lives*.

After the show, *A Raisin In The Sun*, I did the show *Julia* with Diahann Carroll. Julia was an important show, not only because it starred a Black woman in the title role, but because she was also a single, working mother. They didn't have many women, White or Black, playing parts of independent women in those days. It ran from 1968 to 1971. We did about three or four of those shows with her before I got something else.

There were quite a few comedy shows on television now and some were Afro American. I was getting lots of acting jobs and I enjoyed doing them. In 1973, I was about to do that silly Redd Foxx show, *Sanford and Son*. We had known each other for a while. I went to the show one day, and he walked up to me and patted me on the butt.

"What you just hit, belongs to me and my husband. You don't play with me that way. We play with words. Now take that or leave it. Never put your hands on my body again." Redd Foxx had a

Scene from Julia's "Table for Two" episode, with Diahann Carroll.

reputation for being a womanizer, but he never got away with that stuff with me.

During this time, I was studying at Theatre West. That's where I met Carroll O'Connor. I thought he was a lovely man, and we became very good, very close friends. He had written a play he wanted to do with me. The play was about a blind man, played by him, who is sitting on a park bench. A prostitute, played by me, sits next to him, thinking that he is the man she is supposed to meet. It was about mistaken identity. I still have the play. Would you believe it? We started working on it, but never got to do it, because he got that series, *All in the Family*. I liked the play very much, and felt bad, but we would end up working together in 1989 on his show, *In The Heat Of the Night*.

I also have a play that Maya Angelou sent me. That never got done, either.

They also started making a number of movies about Blacks. I would say I appeared in a lot of them and started the action for Blacks in general. I was the "door opener," but I still spoke my mind and kept true to myself.

Now, it was 1974 and I had gone back to work and was filming *Uptown Saturday Night* with Bill Cosby, Harry Belafonte, and Sidney Poitier. It was fun, but Sidney and I didn't get along very well. Harry was a good person and Bill Cosby was a wonderful person. I played Cosby's wife, but I talked a little too country for Sidney. He wanted me to talk "more White."

"Can't you talk better than that," he asked me.

Well, I tried to sound as White and as uncountry as I could. So, when Bill and I started to do our scene, he asked me, "Why are you talking like that?"

"Because Sidney wanted me to," I answered.

"You are playing my wife and you talk like yourself and I'm going to talk like myself. We do the scene the way we want."

And that's what we did.

Me and Bill Cosby.

My Two Big Mistakes, and Marriage, Motherhood, Movies, and TV

The Juggling Years—My Family, and Extended Ones, Too

On the home front, Bill had to have back surgery. He was no help to me at all. I was doing all the work and caring for him. Mama and Earnestine were helping me with my baby. After Bill was off work for about three months, he wanted to go to Texas to see his family. I agreed, so we went to Texas and Arkansas. I saw his sister, nephew, and niece. We stayed there for three days. Since we were so close, I felt we should go see my sister in Pine Bluff. We went to see my family. I also found out that was where Maya Angelou got her first honorary doctorate. My brother-in-law, Dr. Fritz McMurray, was a math teacher at the A&M College in Pine Bluff. We left there to visit my older brother, John Cecil. I think he lived in Tennessee. We had the chance to meet his family. After the visit, we returned home. It had been a nice trip.

My sickness seemed to get worse when we got home, so I started taking more of those pills to keep myself safe while working.

The Veterans Hospital, where Bill worked in the mental health department, had closed. He would only work for Texaco Oil, but they didn't want him to drive. He would work in the office. He didn't like that and I didn't know why. He started begging me to put him in his own business. I didn't know what, but I would do my best to help him. We would see how it went.

On a Monday, I had to go to Chicago for a day, but I had a

seizure and had an accident. I knocked out my front teeth—one was out, root and all, and I had broken the other one—but I went to the dentist and he fixed them so I could make the trip. He told me to be very careful and come back as soon as I got back. The dentist had put the whole tooth back into the gum so I could go to Chicago. When I got back, I went to the dentist after taking William to the nursery. He sent me to another doctor and that doctor put the whole tooth back in. That doctor inserted a post and put another crown over the broken tooth. They fixed it for me, but because of my bad pregnancy, I had lost a lot of calcium in my teeth and had to have lots of root canals.

It was a long day for me. When they finished, I went and got William, fed him, got him ready for bed and I was ready for some sleep. I took the pills. I would always leave Bill's food out so he could warm it and eat when he got home. He'd eat and we would all be in bed, so if I didn't get sick, everything would be all right.

I became tired of Bill begging me for his business. I didn't know what kind of business he was going into. I told him it was for him and William, not me. Don't put my name on it. I told him I hoped he knew what he was doing because I didn't. I had given him some money and hoped he would pay me back.

By then, William was in school. I put him in the first Montessori School that opened because they said it was the best school. Funny being the best. It closed before the year was over. That was bad.

He always wanted a brother and then said he'd take a sister, but as much as I had been through with my condition, I could not have any more children. I was glad I could not. Having him was hard and would last me a lifetime.

Bill enjoyed fishing, but I didn't. Fishing was not my thing. On some weekends, he would go to Mexico with his church friend, Mr. Cooper. The first time they went, they returned with so much fish, it was ridiculous…and I had to clean all of the fish. I gave away some; it was just a mess. I told him if he ever went fishing again, in Mexico or anywhere, he had better have those fish cleaned and filleted. All I would have to do was pack them in bags and give away all I didn't want and put the rest in the freezer.

One time, after we had our family reunion that my mother had planned before her death, I met one of Mama's cousins. He lived in Alaska. For some reason, he caught on to me and asked if I would come to Alaska to spend time with them. He gave me the address and phone number. From time to time, he would call me.

Bill asked me, "Why don't we go to see your cousin in Alaska? You know there is good fishing there and he has asked you to come."

"Okay, we will go on a trip."

I had about three weeks off, so we went fishing. We went through Oregon and we fished for salmon.

We caught a lot of salmon. My cousin had a friend who canned a lot of the salmon for us. They also smoked some of it. It was a big fishing trip and we had salmon for a very long time. He kept the salmon for us while we traveled on to Alaska. When we got to Alaska, it was dark and there was so much ice. We went out on the boat and caught more salmon. It was a beautiful trip. My cousin left Alaska and moved to Arizona. I never went there to see him.

The next time I went fishing with Bill was in Mexico with his friend, Anwar, and his wife. We flew and there was a storm. When we finally landed, we had to get a cab to the fishing resort that we were going to. When we got the cab, the water was so deep, the driver said he couldn't cross. There was a man in a truck, who said he would take us where we wanted to go. Bill and Anwar said, "Let's go." The man got across the first space, but we had further to go. We came to a river and Bill asked the driver if he could make it across that river.

The man said, "Possibly yes, possibly no."

"As far as I'm concerned, it is possibly no," I said.

Anwar and his wife started walking across the river.

"You go ahead. I'll wait here with the man and the truck."

To my surprise, Anwar and his wife had made it safely to the other side. Bill put me on his shoulder and lifted me across. He went back and got the luggage. We went to the resort. It was the end of the season and everyone was gone, except us. They kept the staff there and gave us the best vacation you could imagine. They made food for us night and day. There was a fishing boat every day and when the season was over and our two weeks were up, they got a car to take us to the airport.

One Sunday morning, we were ready to go to church and someone knocked on the door. I thought it was the Jehovah's Witness people because, at that time, they would come to the house, want to come in and study their Bible with you. I would read my Bible and they would read theirs. I wanted to see the difference. This time, it wasn't Jehovah's Witnesses, it was three big girls and they asked if Bill Buckley lived here and I said yes.

They asked to see him and naturally, I told them to come in. I took them in the den where Bill was.

The first thing they said was, "Hi, Daddy. How are you? We just wanted to see you." I thought, *Three*, but I said nothing. I just looked at them because two were older girls and one was younger. They told William they were his sisters. He was glad to have sisters, but it shocked me.

I told them we were on our way to church and asked if they would like to come with us. They said no, they just wanted to see their daddy and said goodbye. We married before I knew Bill had these other children. When he passed away, I found out he had two more.

I realized I had stepchildren and I asked Bill about those kids, but he said to let the past be the past. We had a good life and a son.

They were grown and gone. So, let it be. What could I say? Nothing. The younger girl seemed to be about the same age as William. That was the shock of my life.

I hope no one is mad about my life's story, but I think I married a sick man from the beginning. Bill had to have back surgery about two years after we married. That is something you have to live with because you never get over back surgery. When you think you are well, you may do something or twist or sprain the back and you have back pain all over again. That is something you don't get over.

When I first met the girls, they took to Bill and William, but not me. I believe they thought Bill was making the money, but that wasn't the way it was. He was just another responsibility for me. Later, we found out the second daughter had cancer and was in Kaiser Hospital for a while. Since I had met her, I would go to the hospital to see her when I could, just to show love. When she went home, I never saw her again. I found out months later, she had passed away. I have no information about that.

William met Bill's oldest daughter's son and he was glad; it was like he had a brother. One day she came over to ask if the boy could stay with us because he was going to Dorsey High School. He was a football player. William always wanted a brother and was excited. He said, "Yes, Mama, I'd like that."

"I do not have a bed for him and that means you will have to share the same room and bed," I said. I didn't think that would work, but William said he would sleep in the den and Bill said that would be okay.

I asked, "Do you really want to do that, William?"

He said, "Oh, yes."

Well, I told Phyllis and her son there were things he would have to do.

"I will not be responsible for getting him to or from school," I said. "He will eat supper with us and, if I am not going to work too early, he will eat breakfast with us or cereal. He must keep that bed made up and will have to go home on weekends. He must take his bag of dirty clothes home on the weekend to be cleaned for the next week."

I was working most of the time or going on interviews. I was also a sick woman and I did not need the extra responsibility.

"Oh, we will see to all of that."

Two months later, he was tired of walking from school and riding the bus, but I was not taking on anything. I also thought William was tired of sleeping on that couch.

One day, I was home and Phyllis's son called me from school to pick him up.

"No, I am not starting that. You are going to take the bus or walk like you had been doing." When he got home, I said, "You're not going by the rules. Look at that room. Your dirty clothes are on the floor. I want you to take the bag and put your dirty clothes in it. If you don't want to follow the rules, it is time for you to go home."

I also called his mother and we had our first disagreement. I told her we would not be talking anymore. "Your son must go."

After a little while, she must have called her father, my husband, and I guess he told her it was not his house. He was staying there with me. William was glad to get his bed back. Phyllis picked up her son and left.

Since little Rugie, Earnestine's dog, I had never had a dog. William kept asking for a dog. I took him to a place and he picked himself a dog. It was one of those Golden Retrievers, with the long hair. He wanted the dog but did not want to take care of it. I told him if he wanted a dog, he must take care of it. He didn't and I had to. I ended up attached to the dog and had it for a long time. We had to put the dog to sleep. I cried as if it were human and told William there would be no more dogs at this house. There was not, for a couple of years.

Earnestine's boy had gotten two Doberman Pinschers: a male and female. They had puppies. Rodney, who had the dogs, gave William a puppy. He brought the dog to the house and begged me to let him keep him. I told him he would have to take care of the dog himself and the dog would have to sleep outside. I bought the dog a house. After a while, I had to start walking and taking care of the dog. He was a beautiful black dog. He caught the disease,

My Two Big Mistakes, and Marriage, Motherhood, Movies, and TV

Parvo. If you don't get it treated in three days, it is too late. I thought the dog was sick, but I was working. I told William to make sure he took the dog to the doctor. Of course, the dog hadn't eaten the food William had given him.

The next day after work, when I got home from work and went to the vet, they had put the dog in the death pen and I started crying. The doctor told me to go home. He told me I would have to spray my lawn with bleach. The gardener sprayed my lawn twice. I got rid of the dog house. I have not had another dog since.

When I was not working, I had a lot to do, taking care of Bill and William. I was making it okay, working my butt off. I was sick, but I kept going.

There's another thing that happened two years later. Phyllis's son finished high school and got a scholarship to college. He only stayed in college for one semester and came back home. He was getting married. I didn't know about it, but I found out later. Both William and Bill had gone to the wedding. I found out about it from pictures sent to William and Bill.

In 1993, I had a role in *House Party 3*, playing Aunt Lucy. After the movie, I was home cooking fried chicken and my brother, Frank, called. I had forgotten what I was doing and suddenly I smelled smoke. The fire alarm went off. I hung up the phone and went to the kitchen. I knocked the chicken off the stove and kicked it out the back door—chicken, grease and all. I opened both doors to get the smoke out of the house and started to clean up my house. The

Scene from House Party 3, with Bernie Mac

house was not burning, it was just full of smoke. Because the fire alarm had gone off, the firemen came. It was not that bad, but they came in and opened the door.

"Miss, do you know you've been burnt?" a fireman asked.

"It's not that bad," I replied.

"Yes, it is. We've got to get you to a hospital. Give us a number that we can call someone to let them know where we are taking you."

I gave them Frank's and Bill's number, but I called Bill and told him what had happened. I told him to pick up William. When I got to the hospital, I found out I had bad burns on both hands and would need to have surgery on both hands. Bill found a burn hospital and took me there. I was there for about two months. They had to take skin from the upper leg to put on my hands. Boy, that was a hard surgery, and painful. It took a while to make it through, but time goes on and so do I.

The hospital that I had to go to was quite a distance from my home. It was near to an acquaintance of Bill's. The man who he worked with and who once tried to take Bill's business. His wife was very nice to me and would come to the hospital often to check on me and bring me something to eat.

Before my being burned and being in the hospital, Bill and I would go to their new shop. She had a baby and had fed him three times. The child was crying his tail off and she was getting ready to feed him again. I asked her if she had burped the baby after feeding. She did not know what that was. I took the baby, put him on my shoulder and patted the baby on his back. Out came the gas. The child stopped crying and I told her to always do that. It seemed funny to me that she did not know about burping. Her father was a doctor, I think. Black women always burped their babies, at least in my days, every time they fed the child.

Bill only had a sister, but, for some reason, he loved my brother, Frank, and you know how I felt. Frank talked about marrying a young woman named Mozelle, twenty years younger than him. At first, I was so jealous of Mozelle. I didn't know what to do. After they were engaged, we became the best of friends. When they got married, my son dropped the flowers, dressed in his little black suit. He was so cute.

The day before they got married, Mozelle still didn't have her wedding dress. I went to her house to find out if the man responsible for making it had brought her dress. She was sure that he would bring it. I asked if she wanted me to go and check.

She said, "Oh, no. I believe I will have it on time."

The next day, it was getting close to wedding time. Still no dress. They were getting married in the preacher's house. I don't remember his name. Still no dress. Mozelle was sweating and her hair had gone back. Still no wedding dress. I asked if she wanted me to go to his house. She informed me that it was too late. She wanted her dress to be green and had purchased the green material. Her flowers were green. She had to borrow the minister's wife's gown and it was white.

They got married and at 11:00 a.m., here came the nut with a half-made gown. I was glad he didn't make it on time. I cussed him out. How dare he come walking in here at 11:00 with the half-made dress. I told him to get his butt out of the house and make sure not to send a bill. I told him he had better give a wedding gift for the price of the dress, plus the material, or there would be a good fight.

My brother, Frank, and Mozelle on their wedding day.

Frank and Mozelle went to San Francisco for their honeymoon and were going to stay at a hotel.

Bill suggested, "Let's meet them."

"Okay," I said.

So, we drove to San Francisco and stayed with Bern, her husband and family. William would have company with his cousins. When Frank and Mozelle came to Bern's, they were meeting, laughing and introducing everyone.

Bill and I came out. "Surprise!"

Everyone cracked up, including Mozelle and Frank.

I was taking a lot of pills every day, and they were not working for me. I thought maybe it was my heart. I went to Bill's heart doctor, who said my heart was fine. It was those damn seizures. He said he was sending me to the finest neurologist.

"He's new and if he cannot help you, no one can."

His name was Dr. Panos Marmarelis. He finally started working on my condition with the seizures. It took quite a while to do it, but he worked on it and it seemed I was getting better. He changed some of the medications.

More Film Work, Loss, and Little House On the Prairie

My father passed on December 7, 1979, and was taken back to Arkansas where he was born. Then on February 7, 1981, my mother passed away and she is back home, buried with Papa.

My Two Big Mistakes, and Marriage, Motherhood, Movies, and TV

Time had passed. A couple of years, after my father died, my mother had a stroke. She couldn't talk, but we talked to her just like she could talk. After a while, she started to talk again. William loved to spend Saturday night with Grandma. She let him stay up late at night.

A few years later, she had another stroke and passed away. We had her funeral service here in California, but she, too, wanted us to bury her in Arkansas with Papa. So, the family took her to be with Papa. My older sister, Clem, went with her body and stayed in Hope. She worked as a teacher down there and got married. My mother was about eighty-nine years old when she passed away. I will always remember going to the hospital to see her, and Ezekiel would not let me go into the room because of my condition. So, I did not get to say goodbye to her or see her before she died. Ezekiel was at the door and told me to go home.

Mama was gone and it was tax time for the property in Arkansas. Here came my brother, Hayward, to me. He brought the tax bill and told me to take care of the farmland. Naturally, I started doing what my older brother told me. I did it for many years. I then decided we should divide the bill and each one would pay his share. I guess I was getting too clever. Hayward was buying property in Los Angeles and he felt that if he had to pay taxes on the property, why didn't we just sell the property? He never thought about me paying the taxes all those years. He just thought about himself and his family. I told him I would have to call the rest of the family to find out what they wanted to do.

I paid the taxes for the next couple of years. They all said, if Hayward wanted it, let him have it, but I told him that he would have to pay for it. Now was the time for me to find out the value of the property. That, too, would be a mess for me. I found out that land, the Frierson land, is an important part of Arkansas history. It was always rich in cotton and timber and should go back to being that way. Even the University of Arkansas wanted to protect and conserve it.

I tried to get in touch with Papa's old attorney friend, Robert Lagrones. I couldn't reach him. I thought he may have passed away. His son couldn't help me because he was not a property lawyer. He gave me the name of a woman attorney to do it for me. I had to find out how much the property was worth. I got that done and it was a long process. I was in Los Angeles and had to wait. She called to let me know the value of the property and what to expect. They told me and I told them what they would have to pay. His son wanted to know the lawyer's name so he could call her. I gave him her name. I also got a call from a White man who had a paper plant and wanted to buy the land. I thought if we were going to sell the land, it may as well be to the family. I found all the names of my living brothers and sisters. My twin brothers, my brothers, Mance, John, and Ezekiel were dead. We would divide it equally,

My Two Big Mistakes, and Marriage, Motherhood, Movies, and TV

meaning if one or more were dead, his wife and children would receive payment for his share. If he had only one child, his share would go to the brothers and/or sisters who were still alive. They would do what they wanted and that was what we did.

I kept the mineral rights in the family. My nephew asked me about that. I told him that mineral rights were not a part of the sale. Not that it would ever be of any value, but those rights would always belong to all of Arthur Frierson's children, not just Hayward. All of us.

I was better, but it took my doctor several years to get my condition under control. The last time I spent time in the hospital, I was having petite seizures.

I found out Bill had gone to Prairie View College in his earlier years and played with the Black League. He was a fine player, in both football and baseball. After starting his business, he coached for Baldwin Hills Little League Team. If he saw a young boy walking the streets, he would stop and tell him to have his mother bring him to the park on Saturday. By the time the season started, he had at least twenty little boys. He coached the beginners. When they started, he would take them home. He also had William, trying to teach him, too.

The last year he had almost twenty beginners and he coached those boys and won the city championship. He wanted to take them all the way to the top team that would be the whole four years, but

Baldwin Hills just wanted him to keep finding boys to play on the team. They would practice in the evening on weekdays and play on Saturdays. He made sure the parents knew him and that he would take care of their children. The mothers would bring hot dogs and drinks on Saturday.

I started helping out on Saturdays because I didn't have to work in show business on Saturdays back then. He loved his little champion team and knew he could take them to the top for four years if they had let him keep working with them. Since they hadn't, he stopped coaching but would go by every now and then on Saturday to cheer the boys on. Three of the street boys went on to the pros. There was one boy that played for, I think, Florida. When asked who was his best coach, he said, "Bill Buckley." When asked who that was, he said, "My very first coach in Baldwin Hills."

I was acting as usual and making commercials. I also helped Bill in the shop when I could, and when he needed help. I was also trying to keep William in school.

Bill's company had been going for quite a few years. We had to file bankruptcy three times, but we started over again. His little company had become known overseas. People seemed to like him, but it was the only Black company of its kind and America would not loan him money. It was hard for us.

I went to Chicago in 1990 for a role in a television miniseries, *Brewster Place*, which was the spin-off of the 1989 miniseries *The Women of Brewster Place*, which was based on Gloria Naylor's novel

My Two Big Mistakes, and Marriage, Motherhood, Movies, and TV

*Scene from Brewster Place in 1990.
L to R: Me, Oprah Winfrey, Brenda Pressley*

of the same name. I think it was Oprah Winfrey's first miniseries she produced. We went to her Harpo Studio. I read the script. I only had a couple of lines in the movie and they were near the end, but I was there for four weeks, and it was a long script. I appeared as Patience Jones. I thought they would cut those couple of lines, but they didn't, and thanks to Oprah for the month's work.

Bill's company was asked to make a part that none of the smaller companies wanted to do. He made several sets of them. Come to find out, it's the laser blade. When they found out it would work and they would be needing a lot of them, they took the job from Bill's company and sent it to a big company overseas.

I made another movie, *It's Good to Be Alive*, which was based on the story of Roy Campanella. He was one of our Black baseball players, the catcher. I played the role of his mother. I was told Michael Landon would direct it. I made it to the set and Michael met me. We started talking and laughing as if we already knew each other. That had never happened to me before.

I felt like I knew him, so I told him I was going to tell him something I had never told anyone in this business before.

"It is between you and me… I'm epileptic."

"Don't worry," he said. "I think I am, too."

I don't think he knew what it was. We laughed and he asked, "If it happens, what should we do?"

"Please, don't send me to the hospital."

My Two Big Mistakes, and Marriage, Motherhood, Movies, and TV

I told him if he's not afraid, he could hold me or just lay me on the couch and let me rest until I come to.

"When I come to, ask me my name. If I can't say it clearly, lay me back on this couch and let me rest a little more. When I come to, ask me again. If I'm clear. I'll be ready to do my job."

Could you believe I went right into one just like that? He did just what I told him to do. When I first came to, he asked me my name. I couldn't get it out. He left me on the couch, covered me with something, and told the crew they would do another scene. I slept for about an hour and when I woke up, he asked me my name.

"Michael, you know I know my damn name!"

He said, "She's ready, get her scene ready."

While they were lighting my scenes, he went over my lines with me to make sure I had them down. When everything was set up, he did all my scenes. My day was almost over and he suggested that I rest for a while.

When it was time to go, I went to him to thank him for his help and he asked me if I wanted to be on *Little House on the Prairie*.

"Yes," I said. "Now you know my acting and my condition."

"Yes, I do. I still ask, do you want to be on *Little House on the Prairie*?"

"Of course."

He told me to be at MGM, Stage 15, at five o'clock on Monday morning.

"Okay," I said, then thanked him. I was there and that was my start on *Little House*.

I am grateful to Michael Landon for giving me a chance and not holding my epilepsy against me. Even though my condition never stopped me from doing all the things I needed to, people with epilepsy used to be treated like outsiders and it was something that wasn't talked about much. I thought that was a shame, and when I had the chance, I spoke out about it. I was the first celebrity to raise public awareness about epilepsy, and I did it in an interview with The Los Angeles Times. Can you believe that?

I went on to play Hester-Sue, the school teacher for the blind school. Moses Gunn, who played my friend, Joe Kagan, a prize fighter, was only on for a couple episodes. I always played Hester-Sue. As time passed, my best friend was that mean old woman named Mrs. Olson. Surprising, isn't it?

Scene with Katherine MacGregor, aka Mrs. Oleson

My Two Big Mistakes, and Marriage, Motherhood, Movies, and TV

Me (Hester-Sue) and Karen Grassle (Caroline Ingalls).

**Scene from Little House on the Prairie.
Me with Moses Gunn, who played Joe Kagan.**

My Two Big Mistakes, and Marriage, Motherhood, Movies, and TV

Me and Michael Landon, who played Charles Ingalls.

Ketty Lester

My Two Big Mistakes, and Marriage, Motherhood, Movies, and TV

My brother, Frank, was at the shop when my husband had his second heart attack. He got him to St. Mary's Hospital in Long Beach, where Bill's heart doctor was on staff. I was called and told I had better get there soon, or he would be dead. I had stopped driving and was riding the bus, but I got in the car and made it to the hospital in forty-five minutes. They had given him electric shock treatments and his doctor had helped him make a scratch and had him in surgery by the time I got there. I signed the papers when I made it there. I called Earn and told her to take William with her boys.

Now came the waiting period to see if Bill would make it through. It was his second heart attack, but his first surgery. This was open-heart surgery. Well, he made it. His doctor let me see him, and he looked like he had pipes running from his head to his feet.

Now, it was time for Frank and me to go home and get my boy. This was one of the hardest periods of my life, but somehow, we made it through. Thanks be to God. Bill was in the hospital for about two weeks before we brought him home. I kept him home for about two months before he insisted on going back to work. He lived with that surgery for about fifteen years.

A long time had passed and we were both back to work. This business was hard for both of us. We were Blacks in a White, high-priced world. He went bankrupt, again, and reopened because he had jobs to do and was being sued by the co-owner. The co-owner was doing no work, finding no jobs, just wanted to be paid a salary. He wanted to take the business. We fought this one. Well, we won and didn't pay him anything. So, we started over again. Bill had to change the name of the new company. His customers came back over with him when he called and told them what had happened and the name of the new company, Quality Magnetics. Because of the bankruptcy, Bill had put the business in William's name. He had people that liked him. During the regular season, I would be with *Little House*.

I wanted William to learn to swim, so I took him over to the school where there was a pool. I took him the first day by himself. His teacher said he was doing good. I told Earn to let me take Rodney, my nephew, with us. He would not get in the water, so William came out, too.

I got a movie job that was being made in one of those islands, not Jamaica. I took William with me this time. They loved him there. I was keeping him in the studio, but the young boys came and asked me if they could take him out to the ocean with them. At first, I said, "No," but the director said they would take care of him. They did and taught him how to swim. They would bring him in every so often for me to see him and know that he was safe. We were there for about two weeks or more and then back home.

My Two Big Mistakes, and Marriage, Motherhood, Movies, and TV

Bill was fine, thank God. I had plenty of food in the freezer or he would go out. Sometimes, people would bring him food. When we got home, William started asking to go to the pool. The teacher started putting him in swim races and he would win. The pool closed for some reason that summer and the teacher moved to the valley and taught there. He wanted to take William with him and said he could be a top swimmer, but Bill would not let the man take William. So that was that. It may have taken the opportunity from William to be a top swimmer.

It was my last season on *Little House on the Prairie*. I heard some people talking as I was about to do my scene. They were White and saying, "We'd better be trying to get those Negroes off TV, or they will take over TV like they have taken over sports." I didn't think too much of it.

Michael Landon was trying to buy *Little House*. He was a co-producer and wanted to buy it all, but his partner would not sell his shares. It was near the end of the season and they were taping my last show. I did it and was saying "thank you" and "goodbye" to everyone. I spoke to the co-director and thanked him. He worked with Michael. He remarked, "If you would play more, you would get more."

"I guess I will never get any more because I am a religious, married woman and I don't play that," I snapped. I left.

That was my last day on the show. I went to see my friend, Katherine McGregor, also known as Mrs. Oleson. She told me she was going to the retirement union and I should go there, too. She gave me the name and address of the head lady I was to talk to. I had been with *Little House* for about four years. The show ended on May 10, 1982. Michael Landon went on to do *Highway to Heaven* not too long after. Sadly, though, Michael died on July 1, 1991, of pancreatic and liver cancer.

When I got there, the lady knew all about me and said, "You have been working in this business for thirty years." She wanted to retire me, but since I was not old enough to get my hospitalization, I would have to keep working and earn a certain amount until I was sixty-five years of age. At the time, I was fifty-nine and she told me to get my Social Security early at sixty-two.

She said, "Tomorrow is not promised to any of us."

When I talked to my friend, Katherine, she told me the retirement agent had cancer herself.

When I started *Little House*, I really didn't know the people in the show—no one but Michael. It was that way for quite a while. I was only with the children some of the time and when the scene was over, the children had to go to regular school. There was a special place for the children. I would go to my dressing room.

Finally, Katherine asked me to go to dinner with her. We were finally speaking. I didn't have much to say to her at first, not until we got to know each other. She played her part so well, I thought she was a southern, prejudiced woman, but she wasn't.

When we got to know each other, I asked her how she managed to do that part so well. She said, "From my mother and my aunt. They were just like that."

I don't remember where she came from, but she said she had lived in New York and was a Broadway actress before she got *Little House*. I don't know why, but she could not get another part after *Little House*.

I was able to keep getting parts until I got my hospitalization insurance. We kept in touch with each other, went to see shows, had lunch, went to the movies, but the last time I saw her, she had had some kind of surgery. She was in a rehab place. We spent an hour together and after a while, she moved to the actor's rest home.

The Black shows like *Sanford and Son*, *Good Times*, and *The Jeffersons* started going off, but Bill Cosby had written a show. CBS and ABC were the top two networks. He went to both of those networks and they said they didn't need his show. NBC had fired its president and hired Brandon Tartikoff. Bill told him his show could make him number one and he took it. Bill Cosby's show started and made NBC the number one station. The Cosby Show was important because it showed the life of a Black family who were professionals. Bill Cosby played a doctor, and Phylicia Rashad as his wife, played a lawyer. It was not about life in the projects like *Good Times*, or Black people 'movin' on up,' like in *The Jeffersons*. This Black family could be any family, and everyone related to them because it showed how alike we all are, not how different. That's why the show was so successful. It kept Blacks on the air and NBC stayed number one for seven years.

PART FIVE
The End of Time

As I kept my career going, I tried to help my husband keep his business going too, but 'behind the scenes.' My son, William, had many talents, and many different directions he could choose from. He was, at this time, trying to 'find himself.' Part of his path was to make me a proud grandmother.

William still complained about his eyes, but no one knew what it was. I sent him to Cal Poly, Pomona, but he came home with the same eye problem. He went to City College to take a class in computers since he got good grades. He worked at the shop when he wanted. Once, he took me to do an audition. There were so many people there, he went upstairs. When I finished auditioning, he had met a man who had given him a job making video record promotion films.

William went to Azusa Pacific University. There, they told him he had a dyslexic eye problem. They had found out about it and helped him. He got his BA degree from that university. He wanted his own apartment. He had a girlfriend from Belize who was not a citizen. I told him not to have any children, cover himself, but the next thing I knew she was pregnant. She wanted a baby so that she could become a citizen. I told her that was her problem. I told him not to marry her, just take care of the child. William was the first one to hold the baby. So, I had a grandchild and she was a beautiful baby. They brought the baby to me. I told them to take good care of the baby, but they shouldn't get married. Just take care of the pretty baby.

The girl threatened William that if he didn't marry her, she would take the baby to Belize and he would never see her again. William loved children, so they went to Las Vegas and got married. William started working at the shop and when he was not there, he was with the film people. The girl had told him he had to stay with her five years, so she could become a citizen. I told him he did not have to do that because the baby was already a citizen. He was going to take care of her. I gave him $7,000 for a down payment on a home. I told him to put it in his and baby Tehya's names. That was that, for the time being.

The next thing I knew, there was another baby on the way. I told the girl to get a hysterectomy and she told me they wanted other children. I asked if she was working and she said no. I told her to get a job because they would get nothing else from me. She was not a citizen, having babies. No security in the girl's life.

The End of Time

There was a time when my son was married to his first wife and had the two girls, Tehya and Nayallah. I let them come to the house on Christmas Eve to spend Christmas with us. She had so many toys under the tree for the children that there was no room for gifts for others. After that year, I made sure she didn't do that again.

After dinner, she would change the children's clothes and put on fresh clothes and take them to her families' houses. There they would get gifts. After they were there, Tehya, the oldest girl, was the darker child, was not allowed to play with the other children. She was hurt and one day told me about it and asked if she was different from Nayallah.

"What are you talking about, baby?" I asked.

She told me what her mother had told her and she did not like going to her mother's family's house.

They had told her she was a Negro and they were White. I told her that was a lie. All of you are Black, and she was not to worry about that. Grandma would take care of that. I picked her up and told her that I loved her and that she was beautiful.

One day, her mother came to pick them up. I told the girls to watch television for a minute. "Michelle, you come with me."

We went into my bedroom and I told her if she ever told my granddaughters, either one, that they were different nationalities, her behind was mine. "My son is Black. If you had sex with him

My beautiful granddaughters:

Top:
Tehya Ayana Buckley

Bottom:
Nayallah Buckley
Zaynah Amin Buckley

and had those two kids, they are what he is and if you think you are anything different, you are fooling yourself."

I told her to bring my grandchildren to me. I told both of them that they were Black. I asked their mother if she understood. She had given birth to both and they were sisters. I hugged the grandchildren and told the mother to treat them the same.

Four years later, William filed for divorce. She came to me and I informed her that was between her and William and she could not come to live with me. She put William out of the house. They went to court and the judge told her she could not put a man out of his own home. The judge asked if she was a citizen and explained that she had twenty-four hours to get out of the house. William brought me the keys and asked me to go with her to make sure she leaves. All I could do was wait for her to get out. I opened the door and told her to give me the keys back. Instead, she took the keys and went upstairs and called the police. She had packed all the food and milk from the refrigerator. The police explained that they knew this case and told her to put the milk and food back in the refrigerator and to get her things and get out. The police made her give the keys back to me.

It was court day for them; she didn't show. William had two daughters already and the baby daughter was born after they were separated, and I don't know much about that. I know that she is much younger than the two older girls.

Bill had been given a job to do for a new company and he asked if they could send a print of the part. When Bill got the print, it was complicated for him and he needed to talk to an engineer to help explain it better. The part had several parts to it. Bill was not an engineer himself and it was hard. He knew what it was saying, but it was using a lot of material, which was driving the cost up even more. He needed to know what kind of material, where to purchase it, and how much it would cost. The company should have said what kind of material would be needed, but they didn't.

My sister, Earnestine's, husband was supposed to be an engineer, so Bill asked him for help. Morris came to the shop to discuss the part but decided he did not want to work with us. I guess Bill was not offering him enough money for his advice. Bill wanted Morris because he was family and he was Black; there were no Blacks in the shop, except Bill. It didn't happen, so Bill started looking for another man to look at the part. The man was so happy to get with the company and was willing to start an electrical section in the company. William was not there at the time and I was not there either.

I was not a part of the business and this was the first Black partner. He said he was an engineer. He turned out to be nothing, but he started getting a salary. He raised the price of Bill's new jobs and some of the old ones. He never got the new part started and that's what I thought he was there for. All he talked about was starting his new section and moving to a larger place.

I had met William's new bride, but I didn't really know what she would be like. She said she had a master's degree in accounting, but I never saw her degree, but the children seemed to like her. They seemed to love her more than me. She didn't have children herself. She also said she went to Tuskegee Institute and had various jobs that I didn't know about. Somewhere in this time, she and William had their wedding. We didn't know about it until they invited us to the wedding.

From what I can understand, she had been living with him after his divorce. She knew all about the business. When we turned the business over to him, he told us he could not handle the business without her. She was the accountant. Later, I found all they knew to do was to hire and fire. They didn't know how to find contracts. What the hell had I done?

I did not get involved in his problems if I could help it. I had my bank account and he had his. I paid my church tithes and I guess he paid his. Around this time, the church got a new pastor, who was a lady, Dr. Hines. The church liked her very much and so did we. She was at the church for three years before deciding to run for Bishop. Bill gave her a lot of money to help with her campaign. I didn't mind and I was working and I paid my regular tithes to the church. Bill and I attended the General Conference. That was a first for him. She was one of three Bishops elected, the first woman Bishop for the AME Zion Church. Any time I called her for Bill, she was there for him.

It was during this time that this Navy Captain joined the church. He was an assistant to Dr. Hines. Bill met him. When he found out that Bill owned his own business, the next thing I knew he was at the shop telling my husband that he could get government jobs for him. After he went to the shop, he wanted to buy it. Why all of a sudden would he want to buy the business? All I asked was if he knew the business and how could he get jobs when he doesn't know what to get? The man, Mr. Miller, insisted on buying the business, I encouraged Bill to do it. Mr. Miller offered to buy the business for $2,000,000. He was getting ready to retire from the Navy. I told him that was good and we could retire, too.

I told Bill to let him have it before he knew what he was getting into. Bill knew this business and how hard it was. "If Mr. Miller wants it," I said, "and can get that much from the government, sell it to him. If he needs your help, help him."

Well, in came William. He didn't feel Mr. Miller could run the business and did not want his dad to sell. I asked Bill to pay my house off and I'd be out. They could run this thing. Mr. Miller found out that he had to study to become this salesman. He began to ask Bill for a salary. He was a Black man, too. That's where the trouble all started. Bill was making good money and paid the house off.

As far as the two men were concerned, that was a mistake he made. The Navy man told Bill that he felt William's wife, Chantae, could help with the books and taxes with the company. That's where she came in. She was there and they moved into a bigger building. When they needed help and I was not working, I would help box the parts that I was given, only those parts. I was good at it because I had helped Bill before they had come there. William fired me for packing the wrong parts that I was given. That was fine with me. I stayed home and worked when I got a job. Bill was paying back some of the money I was owed and that was fine with me, too.

I didn't have anything to do with anything at that time. I was not a happy person, but I was satisfied. I had my church and acquaintances and as time passed on, we became friends.

I always did what I could for my sister, Ernestine, all my life. She was good to help me in my early years with my child as well as my mother. There came a time after my brother-in-law, Morris, turned Bill's offer down, that he wanted to take Bill and me to dinner. Something was happening with his property business and naturally, he needed money. He came to us. Well, what were we to do? I didn't say anything. Morris told us what he needed and that it would be repaid within a couple of weeks. I didn't want to, but the Bible says, "Do unto others as you want them to do to you," and it was my sister's husband. Bill loaned him some money and he repaid us. Praise the Lord.

Later, he needed another loan. I really didn't want to do that. I felt that it may become a habit. Well, there went the money. This time it took longer and longer to pay back. Well, we never got the money. Earnestine never mentioned it, naturally, they wouldn't. That was help gone astray.

Farewell, Bill

My son didn't like what the two men were trying to do to his father. Maybe he felt, just like I did, that the stress could kill him. They were setting up separate groups and really doing nothing. William said he would not work that way and left. The people always gave Bill a party on his birthday. He got sick and they brought him home. When they got him home, he could not get out of the truck. William had made it home. I called 911 for an ambulance and they took him to a hospital on Olympic Boulevard. When they checked him and put the thing on his chest, it was a heart attack. I was there this time. They called the San Vincent Hospital and it was filled. He had to be taken to UCLA. Well, it was his third attack and would be his second surgery. Because of his age, UCLA Hospital did not want to do the surgery, but he needed help. He was in pain, so they gave him the surgery and put in stents. Phyllis came there to be with her father and stayed with him and William at night. I would go home and sleep and be there first thing in the morning. That's when I thought I would accept her as a daughter since she helped me. He made it through. He was determined to live and wanted to get out of that hospital.

On the fifth day, when I went to get him, instead of going home to rest, he wanted me to drive him to the shop and to the bank. I said to him, "If you want to die in that shop, that's where it will be." So, I took him there. When we got there, William was working again at the place. We told William he was the head of the company and asked him to go with us back to the bank. He was the legal check signer for the company. Then I took Bill home, cleaned him up, put him to bed and gave him his medicine. I also took mine and we had vegetables and fruit to eat.

Bill wanted to go to Pennsylvania to meet the people who were making the material for his company to make certain parts for another company. They wanted to buy the company. That is where I made my mistake. I should have insisted that he sell to them. William and Chantae didn't want him to sell. They wanted him to sign the business to William. They wanted to run the company. That was okay with me because Bill had to start rehab and I had to get him there.

In the following weeks, Bill had to start rehab at UCLA. We would do that for four weeks and then we had to find our own rehab center. We did and it was one that I could use also. We would go three days a week—Monday, Wednesday and Friday—for one hour. Then I would take him to the shop for at least two hours. He wanted to do that.

I had acted, made commercials and got reruns enough to earn my healthcare, so I did not have to work unless I wanted to. Bill was sick and I took care of him. That was a big enough job doing that. We were always taking him to the doctor.

There was a time when Phyllis was moving to Dallas, Texas, with her daughter. The daughter was going to college and Phyllis's job was opening an office there. We went on a trip to Texas by train. Bill didn't like airplanes, not only because of the stents, but he always had to have a doctor's card or something. By going on the train, he could sit up or lay down when he wanted to. The trip was nice and we made it back. Everything went well.

When we got home, Phyllis would always call Bill. I understood and didn't make a fuss about it. That was their business, not mine.

He was always going to the doctor. He had some kind of eye infection and had to go to a specialist. He made a joke about how my father could fix his eye for him. We laughed. My father would do anything and had told my husband about it when we were down home. His eye kept hurting and he had used everything he knew to stop it from hurting. One night, he went to the barn and got a little turpentine. He came back and told Mama to drop a little drop in his eye. She asked if he was sure he wanted this done and he said, "Just a little bit." She did what he asked. He went to bed and the eye stopped hurting. When he woke up, he couldn't see out of it.

Bill said, "I think I'd better go to the doctor."

"Yes, because he forgot to tell you he put his eye out."

I took Bill to the specialist, who took a needle and shot him in the eye. He also gave him laser treatments, which took the redness from the eye.

Despite all our mistakes in our lives and almost forty-nine years of marriage, Bill had become a deeply religious man. He had read the Bible through twice and he believed in God. He still wanted to work, and so did I. I was still singing spirituals in the church. As time passed on, we were getting closer. He was sicker and older and there were always problems with him. He had diabetes and I had to take better care of him, testing his levels for diabetes and getting his medications.

I was okay and my doctors had my seizures under control. Bill was not too well, but he wanted to go on another trip to Texas. If he wanted to, that was what we would do. It had been over a year and he wanted to see his nephew, niece, and his daughter. Well, that was okay with me. William and his new wife had taken over the shop. Well, we went, but the trip was not as good as the first. He was sick, but he saw everyone. They came to the hotel most of the time.

I was glad to make it home. On Monday, after we got home, Bill wanted to go to his rehab and insisted on driving himself. He was driving faster than I drove. We got there and he couldn't get out of the truck. I ran and got his nurse. When they came outside, they took his pulse, called an ambulance and back to the hospital we went. This time it was St. John's and he'd suffered another heart attack. The third surgery changed two stents, but they had to leave in twenty percent of the blockage. He was a tough man and made it through. He started his rehab, which lasted from October until about July, prior to his death.

On the last trip to Texas, I had wanted to go to Pine Bluff to see my sister, Eva Pearl. I had bought my tickets to take the bus from Little Rock to Pine Bluff. I had called her daughter, who didn't want me to come. I didn't want to be a bother to anyone. I just wanted to see my sister very much. I like to see the person while they are alive. I had not seen her in about seven years. She had cancer. I could have helped her take care of Eva.

About two years before, I had taken care of my brother, Frank. He had cancer, too. I cared for him every day and fed him. My sister, Earnestine, would sleep at the apartment at night. I would take care of him during the day. When I got my family fed and William off to school, I was there with Frank all day. It was no big deal. We were family. I had called my sister, Earnestine, and told her to come. I didn't want to be alone when he passed. I could not go home, I just felt like it was the end for him and I wanted to be with him.

With my sister, Eva, I knew she would die. I just wanted to see her alive. Since her daughter didn't want me to come, I made

The End of Time

sure Bill made it to Texas to see his family. Eva's daughter lived in Dallas. It seemed as if she could have called me, but she didn't. This was October 2012, and Eva died in February of the following year. My sister, Amanda, died the same week. When she died, Amanda's daughter came to San Francisco for a memorial service and we all attended.

Bill was hurting and we went to his heart doctor, who said he would not do another surgery on him. "He's too old."

This was the time in our lives that I had hoped we would be together, enjoying life and getting to really know each other, but it was the end.

All he could do was through medication. We left the doctor's office and Bill wanted to go to the shop and the bank. Bill wasn't feeling well, so we had to go to the hospital where his doctor was on staff. When we got there, we found he had pneumonia. They kept him in the hospital for three weeks. Then he was sent to a nursing center for rehab, where he stayed for two weeks. I decided I would bring him home. I had a day nurse and a night nurse. He only lived for two months. I believe it's better to be at rest with God than to be suffering.

I called his daughter to let her know he was dying. She and her daughter came and they called their stepsister in Oakland, who also came. His niece and nephew came after he passed. I was proud of the help I got from my son and his new wife. In a few days, he was buried. We were married forty-nine years.

Ketty Lester

I met this man a long time ago, you see,

He was not what I hoped that he would be

Maybe I was not what he thought I would be either,

But we have lived for all these years together, in spite of the troubles

He worked real hard, in spite of his health,

I did what I could to try to help.

Well, he's gone now and frankly speaking, I don't feel lonely at all

This old house has brought us this far

I hope I will be able to keep it just for the joy

Goodbye, my Bill, I will see you later

It may not be that long before we are back together.

*My husband,
Bill James Buckley*

PART SIX
Yesterday, Today, and Tomorrow

Nobody Told Me the Music Business Changed

To me, show business was not as easy as it seemed and was never a guarantee but just luck. You would be taken advantage of if you were not strong enough. I had been considered one of the "door openers" for my people, especially in commercials and in the television acting field. I say to anyone, don't let the sun go down with disrespect for yourself lying in your path. Always have pride in yourself, even if no one else has it. Remember, no one can make you do, make you say, make you drink anything you don't want to. I was never a big star, never made big money, but those that knew me respected me. I do unto others as I want them to do to me. Most of us can't say that and as God says, *Love ye one another*. I don't say I love everyone, but I try. I am always willing to forgive even when I don't always forget.

My records were still being sold, and RCA had sold just about all of my records to a German company named BMG, and BMG was bought by Sony. As far as I know, that's where my records are now. My record, "Love Letters," has also been in three movies: *The Color Purple, Blue Velvet,* and *Love Letters,* which were not my lyrics. Many people have covered the song, like Elvis Presley in 1966 and Allison Moyet in 1987 in the United Kingdom, where my version reached number 1 on the charts and stayed there for a year.

I was asked to come to Nashville, Tennessee, to film a show with lots of rock and roll singers and writers. They said they wouldn't do it without me. The show was part of a series that had live conversation and music with a number of rock and roll music makers of the 1950s and 1960s. There were rare, original performances of 52 songs from 37 artists. They wanted me to be one of those 37 people, sitting in a big circle, sharing our stories, and they wanted me to sing "Love Letters!" I didn't want to do it, but the producers liked my record, so I went. The only artists I knew of were Mary Wilson and Dee Dee Sharp, but I never met them before. I still didn't understand why they wanted me there so bad, but the producer told me, "You are such an impressive singer and performer. 'Love Letters' needs to be a part of this series."

Well, I didn't know about how those rock and roll musicians would feel about me. They had a very fine band, led by Steve Jarrell, to back up all the musicians. I was so nervous that I said I needed to take my time. I still was not sure if I wanted to sing. I was reassured that I didn't have to sing if I didn't want to, so they let me sit on the sidelines and just watch everyone on the first day.

On the second day I felt like I was ready to try. Steve, Spig Davis, who was the keyboard player, and I went backstage to rehearse. We found a piano and ran though the song just one time. I asked Steve if he thought I was ready, and he said, "Ketty, *you* are *ready!*"

I sat with all those wonderful musicians and listened to their stories and their songs. I shared my story with them about having my epileptic seizure on the set of *It's Good to Be Alive,* The Roy Campanella Story, how wonderful Michael Landon was to me, and how he invited me to work on *Little House*. Now, it was my turn to sing "Love Letters."

Well, I stood up, and I sang my song, and when I had finished, I looked out at the audience, and for some reason, everyone, even the band, was in tears. Then, they gave me a standing ovation. I could not believe it! Everyone was so deeply touched by my song that they actually had to stop taping and break for dinner so that they could compose themselves.

Now, I don't know for sure, but I think they all came to tears because they truly felt my pain.

But it was true. Everybody was crying, even Charley Monk, the CBS executive.

He stood up and said, "What's everyone crying about? And why am *I* crying, too?"

The producer of the show said, "Because you just witnessed Ketty Lester's "Love Letters Straight from Your Heart."

I met Mary Wilson, whom I had never met before. She used to be with The Supremes. She came up to me and wrapped her arms around me.

"Why are you crying?" I asked her.

"The first time I heard your song was the day I found my boy dead in my pool." She said she couldn't say why everyone else was crying, but she knew she could not help herself.

Well, "Love Letters" was done in just one take. I'm glad I decided to do it. I was there for three days, and I met a lot of very fine people and made some very good friends.

I still hear from Steve Jarrell. He's become a lifelong friend. He is still a deejay on the radio and he calls me on my birthday from time to time. Every year, we talk, and he plays my song.

The last recording I ever made was for Dave Bell and Jim Shaw. Their company was Mega Records. They wanted a religious version of "One Day at a Time," but the song that became number 32 was "She Never Heard of Anyone Called Jesus." Dave was pushing "One Day at a Time." He even booked me at the Grand Ole Opry, a concert hall in Nashville, Tennessee. I went there, but Mega didn't have enough production money.

The music business doesn't work like it used to at all, and if it was up to me alone, I wouldn't know nothing about how things work these days, and I wouldn't even know some things about my own career. Can you imagine that? But, today, I am blessed to be meeting different people and learning different things about myself I never knew. For example, I would never have known about how Sony Records ended up with all my tapes and records.

Back in the 50s and 60s, lots of little record companies were putting out music by folks like me. Seems that as the popularity of our music was growing, all these little companies were getting bought and sold.

Another thing I did not know about was that I had been nominated for a Grammy back in 1962. You see, it makes sense that I wouldn't know because I was still in New York and loved very deeply by Carlo. I didn't have proper management. When I left New York, I was broken hearted and came right back to my Mama's house. I went on hiatus. I didn't see anyone in the business and I kept to myself, just going to church and cooking and taking long walks. I didn't go to any of the old places where people knew me. I just needed to heal my soul from my break with Carlo.

If you had told me back then that I was nominated, I wouldn't have believed it, and to tell you the truth, when I heard about it all these years later, I still didn't believe it. It took a lot of talk and hard work by my friend, Nancy.

She called one day to tell me about the Grammy nomination and I told her, "Don't believe everything you read on the Internet. I wasn't nominated for no Grammy. Nobody told me nothing about that." But Nancy insisted it was true and she was going to prove it to me. She knew I needed to see something real, not just something on the Internet, so Nancy went ahead for about 2 months trying to get me some proof. Then one day, proud as can be, she called to tell me she gone and done it. Nancy told me it was listed on the web site of the National Recording Academy. She started calling and emailing them every day explaining that she needed to get me a letter and certificate, and with the help of a nice young man named Ralph Oliverez, she got the Academy to find, and send the certificate. Well, I finally believed Nancy, because she made sure that I could hold the certificate in my hands, and you can see a copy of it right here in this book.

The Fifth Grammy Awards, hosted by Frank Sinatra, took place on May 15, 1963 and nearly 60 years later, a letter arrived at my house proving that I was nominated for "Love Letters", along with Lena Horne (Lena...Lovely and Alive), Diahann Carroll (No Strings), Sandy Stewart (My Coloring Book), and Ella Fitzgerald, who won, with "Ella Swings Brightly with Nelson." It is an honor to know how much my record was appreciated and that I had, and still have fans. It keeps me going while I am struggling to get this book out.

Yesterday, Today, and Tomorrow

May 16, 2019

Ketty Lester
5118 West 20th Street
Los Angeles, CA 90016

Dear Ms. Lester,

It is my pleasure to confirm your GRAMMY Nomination.

You were nominated in the Best Solo Vocal Performance, Female category for your reco Letters" at the 5TH GRAMMY Awards which took place on May 15, 1963.

Congratulations on this well-deserved recognition by the voting members of the Record

Best regards,

Bill Freimuth
Chief Awards Officer

Because the music industry doesn't take care of so many of us anymore, we have to do what we can do for ourselves. If it wasn't for my friend Nancy, I wouldn't even know where to start. Even though there's a lot of information on the Internet about me that isn't true, it *is* good for some things. I have a profile on Facebook, and Instagram, my music is on Spotify, and I have my own website too. I thank God for them, and for Nancy's help, because through these things, and this book, I can stay in touch with my fans, and it keeps my music alive.

Doing Unto Others, Like The Bible Says

It's not the end of my life. I'm still doing things. My life is lonely, but I still go to church with people there. The people from *Little House* call me now and then. Katherine MacGregor left her apartment to live at the Motion Picture and Television Fund retirement community in Los Angeles, a rest home for entertainers, where she later died on November 14, 2018, at the age of ninety-three.

I'm still trying to do something to help my family. There's only three of us still alive in this big family. I lost my sister, Berniece, a few years ago. Mattie lives in San Francisco, but she is sick. Her young daughters take care of her. Earn is here and I try to keep a check on her. I have had to try to help my son, but I'm about out of money. I'm trying to do what I can for everyone, but I must start trying to help myself. I hope I get this book done if it is the will of God. All I can do is trust Him.

My son has two sons, so I have five grandchildren now. I hope they do well and they will make it through these tough times. It is hard now. That's why I'm still trying to do all I can. I hope this book will sell, but I don't know if the people of my day are still alive *(inner laughter)*, but I am.

Since Bill passed away, I haven't heard from Phyllis. I do hear from his nephew and I have heard from my older brother's son, John Cecil Frierson. I have been invited to Elvis Presley's birthday adventures. The first one I went to was at a club in North Hollywood. I had never been there before. Then they wanted me to sing. I sang "Love Letters" and that's all. They wanted me to sing more.

But I did not want to get involved in that too much because the musicians were not good players. They played by ear, not readers. They didn't play my kind of music and I really don't know the kind they play, so I think I am outclassed and I stay away from it. The lawyer who asked me to come to that club called again the next year and invited me to a theater in Hollywood.

They were raising money for the Republican political party.

When he told the man I was there, he asked me to sing, but I declined. I haven't heard from the lawyer anymore. They did it just because Elvis put "Love Letters" on one of his albums with the same arrangement as mine. Just like mine. The disc jockeys did not play his version, only mine. Pat Boone also put my "Love Letters" on his album, but they didn't play his.

Everybody will use you if they can get away with it. I have been used vocally too much and I don't go for that.

It seems to me the world has changed for the worst. If we could change this world the way it should be changed, all would be different, especially about love. It would be so exciting to see the love and learn about different people. Accepting them as they are, not because they are the same color as you are.

God made everybody and everything a little different. A little different in language, a little different in color. Just look at the fish, the birds, the animals; everything is different and beautiful in its own way. Nobody could do that but God. God is love. We should try to say "I love you" every day because tomorrow may never come. Look what a precious thing you passed away.

We fight for and live for so many things in life. We must do those things when we can because we are not promised tomorrow. Look again at what we have missed. We didn't say "I love you." There's a lot of things in life we hope and pray for and we had better do it while we can. Suppose tomorrow doesn't make it. Look again at what we have missed. There are things that we try to forget.

We should say what we want to say today. Love should be in that saying. Ask the question you want to ask today, or you may never get the answer you wanted to know. So, you missed out on something special. You may want to know about the Bible, but if you don't read it today, tomorrow may be too late. Do you want to know who God is? Well, God is love and, every time you say love, you are remembering the Spirit of the Holy One, God. May the Spirit bless you all.

I love you all.

Looking After My Family, Looking After Myself

Since becoming older and deciding to write my memoir, it is not easy to tell all the things that happened and the mistakes I have made. I do hope my son and his family they are well and happy. I hope my son's health will be good. I hope he is taking his medication. I hope his wife is helping him, as I helped my husband. He has a big family to take care of—three girls and two boys. I can't help them anymore. I have helped all I could and now I must take care of myself. I am alone, but I'm okay. I have always been independent.

We learned so much in our world. We made such big mistakes, but it is something that we have to live within life, or you never learn.

The last time I came home from New York, I had a lot of time to think, be alone and sing a little, mainly in church. At the time, my church was trying to buy a parsonage. I decided to do a concert for the church. Reverend C. D. Tolliver was our pastor. I decided to do what I could to help pay for the parsonage. I started planning a concert at the church and all the proceeds of the concert were to be put on the parsonage. It turned out very well. I ended up making over $12,000 dollars which I donated to the church.

My pianist, Lincoln Mayorga, wrote my opening song. He played for me. Ray Brown was my bass player and was known at the time as one of the greatest stand-up bass players. Earl Palmer was on drums. He was with me on "Love Letters." Harold Pittman was on the organ and was the director of our choir. Lincoln was a classical pianist and played Beethoven's "Sonata" for piano in C sharp. He played Opus #22 #21. The musicians all played for free.

I found out later that Lincoln had recorded the concert, made a record of it and put it on his company called Sheffield RLab. It was called *Ketty Lester in Concert*. I guess it turned out okay for him and a good payment on the parsonage. I was glad to do that, but I don't know how that record got on Sony.

I kept working and making commercials when I could. I heard that Smokey Robinson had become a minister and was at one of the airport hotels on Sundays. I decided to go to his church. I don't think he knew anything about the Bible, and he was singing his own songs.

He recognized my presence and that was where I met the great Smokey Robinson. He asked me to come back to the church, but I hadn't heard anything that touched me religiously. I asked him,

"What would I sing here?" He told me I could sing my own songs or any song. I told him I always sang religious songs whenever I sing in the church. I promised I would try to make it back, but I never did.

Then I heard that Della Reese had become a preacher and I decided to visit her church. She tried to do better. If you are not touched by God, you are not a preacher. She tried to talk about the Bible, but she was very long-winded and really didn't know the Bible well. I didn't go back there, either. I stayed with the AME Zion Church and I am still with them.

I finally got a call from the agent for the girls from the *Little House on the Prairie*. I didn't really know them, but I did get a chance to meet the children who were grown. It was interesting to see them all and I have not seen them since.

After a few months, I got a call from an old acquaintance of mine who had moved into the Motion Picture & Television Fund (MPTF) rest home for actors. One of the MPTF people came to my home. Now, Wright King had already introduced me to the woman who got him in. She was not that interested in me. I heard I should not go into that place. But being nosy that I am, I decided to check them out. I knew I had never heard of a Black being in that place and had been told by someone in the union that they did not bring in Blacks. But I wanted to see for myself.

First, they sent me a social worker and we talked. Then, they sent me this woman named Evisha Clark. I guess she was the LCSW (Licensed Clinical Social Worker), which I didn't know what that meant. She was expecting a child and my representative was named Jamie Grauman. She told me all the papers I needed to send them. Well, I sent them all she had asked me to send.

She told me I had sent more papers than most of the people that were there. They had no reason not to take me in. I didn't want to go in, I just wanted to find out. Then, I met another woman at MPTF and her name was Wendy Garfinkel, who was supposed to be an MSW (Masters of Social Work.) I didn't know what that was either or what it represented.

Now Wendy was just sure that I could afford to live there. She invited me out to see the place. She had a driver pick me up and bring me to the place. The driver explained that he did not want to leave me there.

"This is a White place, and you are not safe," he said.

"Don't worry. They will have to get me back home," I said and he left.

Wendy met me at the door and showed me all around the place. It was tacky to me. I did not see one Black person in the place. They were fixing the big swimming pool and even had a movie theatre. I'm sure I wouldn't have seen any of the great Black movies that are out now. They took me to lunch and we talked. I was introduced to a man who knew me. He was an old disc jockey who knew I had made "Love Letters," and he started crying.

They let me know that day that I would not be accepted at the home. I didn't like the place. The rooms were so small and the place was so far away. The place was not the way I was used to living. They also told me to never call Wendy again. That was fine with me. That was that. It was an interesting day and they got me a driver to take me home. I haven't heard from any of those fools and don't want to. They returned all of my papers.

My sister, Berniece, was hit by a drunk driver and her hips were broken. She was given money, but Berniece did not know to put the money in proper places. She had it everywhere. My sister, Amanda, called me, as always, to find out where all the money was. I found out where all the money was, in about five different insurances. I had placed it all in one insurance. I took it to San Francisco, showed it to Berniece, Amanda and Mattie and gave them the papers.

I told Berniece to always keep your money in one place. Eventually, Berniece had to go into a home; they used that money to pay for her care.

I am happy and hope I will be until God takes me away.

I have my two nephews—Keith and David Frierson—who will try to help me if I call them. Keith will take me to the doctor when I call to let him know the date and the time. David calls sometimes to take me to dinner, but I depend on Keith.

I also spend a lot of time visiting and caring for my sister, Earnestine, and her husband. They are in a rest home and I try to visit them as much as I can. My sister, Mattie, is in a rest home, too. I think she is fine. Her two daughters are watching over her.

Eventually, I sold my house. I still had to go through the power of attorney that William had me sign with him. I finally got the power, sold the house, paid all of the bills and I took what was left, which is what I am living on right now.

I am a true believer in the Bible. The Bible says that you reap what you sow. That means if you do wrong, eventually wrong will return to you.

PART SEVEN
All My Love, Ketty

Now, I cannot stop writing this without a deed or word to my friend, Josephine Drake, who has not only been my friend, but has helped me. She typed my autobiography and other things I have asked her to do. She has never turned me away. If I ever get this published, I owe her so much for what she has done to help me. I love her with all my heart and I want the world to know that. She is my closest and dearest friend. When my husband was alive, her husband, Charles, and my husband, Billy James Buckley, were close friends.

This is how I feel today. One of my regrets is that I never apologized to Carlo for what I said when we separated because I never answered the letters. As far as my husband is concerned, I will take my memories of him to the grave with me. We will be together then.

I have experienced a hard time in my life, enjoyed a very loving time in my life, a fearful time in my life and also a sense of peace.

My marriage was not the greatest, but I accepted it, even with the mistakes we made by doing it. We had a son and that was good. But it was all a part of life. We stayed married for forty-nine years and that was good. We had some good times; the vacations, the fishing.

Dr. Maya Angelou was an interesting acquaintance. Even though we did not remain friends, I still had great respect for what she had accomplished. She was snooty acting, but I knew her when.

I do think Dorothy Shay was a help to me. It was interesting, but I found out that it was not easy for an entertainer to manage another entertainer. She did get me an acting part on the television show, *Days of Our Lives*. She and the owner of the show, Betty Corday, were responsible and there was no agent involved. Then we had the separation; she was doing her job and I was doing my job. That's when the mix up came with the recording.

But she still got me the first New York nightclub job and I had the wide bottom pants that I had designed for me. I ask the question often: Did she and her designer take that from me? I was put with the GAC agency and I never saw Dorothy Shay again. It was just me in a big city I knew nothing about, and no manager, just a new agent. Boy, that was a fearful and lonely time. I had to go where the agent sent me to eat and live. So, I did.

That's when I met Cab Calloway and my friend, Audrey, and Carlo, the man I fell in love with. I didn't know anything about him then, but now I do. Carlo's family dates back to the thirteenth century and I don't even know what part of Africa my background comes from. Both parts of my family were so mixed up, you would not even know what was what anyway. How could I mix into that world?

It seems to me that life is a funny thing. On one side, I was a "door opener," making a way for other Black women in show business. On the other side, seems like there was one door that could never open, and that door led to a full, real life with Carlo. Still, when we were together, we had a great life. I knew I loved him and I believed he loved me. The idea of us having a child then gave me great fear. That's why I never answered his letters.

I have seen the world change, and the TV, music, and film industry change with it. Black people have their own production companies, and stories about the Black experience are being told now more than ever. We have come a long way, but there is still a long way to go. For example, in my opinion, that movie *Hidden Figures* should have won best picture, best cast and best woman star performance. Denzel Washington should have gotten the Oscar for best actor and Viola Davis for supporting actress for that movie called *Fences*. I believe the White actors know they have competition. I'm glad for the actors and actresses, even if they don't know what I did, it doesn't matter. However, it matters when people don't vote for the right person and don't vote every voting chance.

When there were those of us who died, were put in jail, and bitten by dogs for that right, and people don't use that right…it's sad.

As I have been writing this, I'm seeing that it's more than just the story of my life. It's my Love Letter to you. I hope that I have shown you what life was like back in the day, what the struggles were, not just for me, but for all Black folks, and all women, too. I want you to know that it pays to be strong, maybe even headstrong, like they used to call me. You don't have to do anything you don't want to do to get where you need to go. Just have faith in yourself, and faith in the Lord, and never, ever make compromises. You need to hold on to that one big love in your life, no matter what anyone says, and keep it close to your heart, and above all, always, always be yourself. So, I will close my bio with this song to the two men in my life—my first love and my husband. This song was recorded by my favorite singers: Billy Holiday and Eartha Kitt, written by Don Raye and Gene De Paul. The song is "You Don't Know What Love Is."

> You don't know what love is
> Until you've learned the meaning of the blues
> Until you've loved a love you've had to lose
> You don't know what love is
> You don't know how lips hurt
> Until you've kissed and had to pay the cost

All My Love, Ketty

Until you've flipped your heart and you have lost
You don't know what love is
Do you know how lost heart feels
At the thought of reminiscing
And how lips that taste of tears
Lose their taste for kissing
You don't know how hearts burn
For love that cannot live yet never dies
Until you've faced each dawn with sleepless eyes
You don't know what love is
You don't know how hearts burn
For love that cannot live yet never dies
Until you've faced each dawn with sleepless eyes
You don't know what love is
...Love, Ketty

PICTORIAL

Me being recognized by the Los Angeles City Council.

William, me, and Bill.

My nephew, Keith Frierson

Pictorial

Me at the Grand Ole Opry.

Ketty Lester

Pictorial

Me with Pearl Bailey

Scene from The Little House on the Prairie

The Little House on the Prairie Reunion
Top: Dan McBride, Lucy Lee Flippen, Alison Arngrim
Bottom: Rachel Lindsay Greenbush, Me, Wendi Lee Turnbush

Pictorial

Scene from Sanford & Son, 1993

On the set of Little House on the Prairie

Me with Pearl Biiley

Ketty Lester

Scenes from Porgy & Bess

Pictorial

FILMOGRAPHY
Ketty Lester's Roles in Television and Movies
(in chronological order)

1957: "You Bet Your Life" hosted by Groucho Marx (TV Series)

1960: Amerikanische Impressionen (TV Short)

1962-1968: American Bandstand (TV Series)

    Episode #12.13 (1968) ... Herself

    Episode #9.43 (1966) ... Herself

"The Debut of The New AMERICAN BANDSTAND 1966" (1965) ... Herself

    Episode #5.256 (1962) ... Herself

    Episode #5.165 (1962) ... Herself

1962-1965: Thank Your Lucky Stars (TV Series)

    Episode #9.11 (1965) ... Herself

    Episode #3.39 (1963) ... Herself

    Episode #3.5 (1962) ... Herself

1964: That Regis Philbin Show (TV Series)

    Episode #1.48 (1964) ... Herself

    Episode #1.6 (1964) ... Herself

    Episode #1.2 (1964) ... Herself

1964: The Steve Allen Playhouse (TV Series)

    Episode dated 8 October 1964 (1964) ... Herself

1965-1966: Where the Action Is (TV Series)
   Episode #2.217 (1966) ... Herself
   Episode #2.138 (1966) ... Herself
   Donovan & Miss Ketty Lester (1965) ... Herself
   Episode #2.1 (1965) ... Herself
1965: Juke Box Jury (TV Series)
   Episode #1.330 (1965) ... Herself - Panelist
1965: Ready, Steady, Go! (TV Series)
   Episode #3.14 (1965) ... Herself
1965: The Eamonn Andrews Show (TV Series)
   Episode #2.9 (1965) ... Herself
1965: Hollywood a Go Go (TV Series)
   Episode #1.46 (1965) ... Herself - Singer
   Episode #1.37 (1965) ... Herself - Singer
1965: Hollywood Discotheque (TV Series)
   Episode #1.6 (1965) ... Herself
   Premiere (1965) ... Herself
1964-1965: Shindig! (TV Series)
   Episode #2.1 (1965) ... Herself - Singer
   Episode #1.8 (1964) ... Herself - Singer
1965: Shivaree (TV Series)
   Episode #1.32 (1965) ... Herself
1966: The Lloyd Thaxton Show (TV Series)
   Episode #4.215 (1966) ... Herself
1967: George Jessel's Here Come the Stars (TV Series)
   Carl Reiner (1968) ... Herself

Filmography

1968: The Woody Woodbury Show (TV Series)
Episode dated 12 March 1968 (1968) ... Herself
Episode dated 16 January 1968 (1968) ... Herself

1968: Pat Boone in Hollywood (TV Series)
Episode #1.85 (1968) ... Herself

1968: Uptight (Movie)
Alma

1969: Win with the Stars (TV Series)
Ketty Lester/George Jessel (1969) ... Herself - Celebrity Contestant
Ketty Lester/Richard Long (1969) ... Herself - Celebrity Contestant

1969: The Bill Cosby Show (TV Series)
A Girl Named Punkin (1969) ... Cathy

1969: Julia (TV Series)
From Whom the Wedding Bell Tolls (1969) ... Rita Hopkins
The Undergraduate (1969) ... Rita Hopkins
Love is a Many Sighted Thing (1969) ... Rita Hopkins
Home of the Braves (1969) ... Rita Hopkins
Matchmaker, Break Me a Match (1969) ... Rita Hopkins

1969: That Girl (TV Series)
The Defiant One (1969) ... Mrs. Ellis

1969: Green Acres (TV Series)
Retreat from Washington (1969) ... Receptionist
The Birthday Gift (1969) ... Operator

1969: The F.B.I. (TV Series)

Eye of the Storm (1969) ... Mrs. Shepard

1970: Here Come the Brides (TV Series)

A Bride for Obie Brown (1970) ... Johnnie Mae

1970-1973: Love, American Style (TV Series)

Love and the Games People Play/Love and High Spirits/Love and the Memento

Love and the Single Husband/Love and the Stutter (1973)

Love and the Champ/Love and the Pen Pals (1970) ... Martha

1971: Room 222 (TV Series)

The Long Honeymoon (1971) ... Mrs. Ellis

Mr. Bomberg (1971) ... Mrs. Ellis

1972: Blacula (Movie)

Juanita Jones

1972: The Rookies (TV Series)

Time is the ire (1972) ... Tina

1972-1973: New Temperatures Rising Show (TV Series)

Panic in the Sheets (1973) ... Nurse Ferguson

Witchcraft, Washington Style (1972) ... Nurse Ferguson

Operation Fastball (1972) ... Nurse Ferguson

1973: Sanford and Son (TV Series)

The Infernal Triangle (1973) ... Judy Edwards

1973-1975: Marcus Welby, M.D. (TV Series)

Public Secrets (1975) ... Betty Fisher

The Fatal Challenge (1974) ... Thelma Walters

A Joyful Song (1973) ... Nurse Walsh
1974: Uptown Saturday Night (Movie)
Irma Franklin
1974: Salty (TV Series)
For the Love of Clancy (1974) ... Maggie
1975: It's Good to Be Alive (TV Movie)
Roy Campanella's Mother
1975: The Streets of San Francisco (TV Series)
Endgame (1975) ... 1st Prostitute
1975: Harry O (TV Series)
Street Games (1975) ...Sally Jackson
1975: The Prisoner of Second Avenue (Movie)
Unemployment Clerk
1976: Days of Our Lives (TV Series)
Episode #1.2708 (1976) ... Helen Grant
1976: Louis Armstrong – Chicago Style (TV Movie)
Mrs. Thomas
1976: Adventurizing with the Chopper (TV Movie)
Cousin Bea
1976: Hunter (TV Series)
Susie
1977: Sugar Time! (TV Series)
Fear of Heckling (1977) ... Lillian
1977: The Waltons (TV Series)
The Stray (1977) ... Mrs. Thomas

1977-1983: Little House on the Prairie (TV Series)
- A Child with No Name (1983) ... Hester-Sue Terhune
- Home Again: Part 2 (1983) ... Hester-Sue Terhune (credit only)
- Home Again: Part 1 (1983) ... Hester-Sue Terhune
- Love (1982) ... Hester-Sue Terhune
- The Empire Builders (1982) ... Hester-Sue Terhune
- The Return of Nellie (1982) ... Hester-Sue Terhune
- Little Lou (1982) ... Hester-Sue Terhune
- Rage (1982) ... Hester-Sue Terhune
- Welcome to Olesonville (1982) ... Hester-Sue Terhune
- A Promise to Keep (1982) ... Hester-Sue Terhune
- Second Chance (1982) ... Hester-Sue Terhune
- A Christmas They Never Forgot (1981) ... Hester-Sue Terhune
- Wave of the Future (1981) ... Hester-Sue Terhune
- Dark Sage (1981) ... Hester-Sue Terhune
- The Reincarnation of Nellie: Part 2 (1981) ... Hester-Sue Terhune
- The Reincarnation of Nellie: Part 1 (1981) ... Hester-Sue Terhune

www.ingramcontent.com/pod-product-compliance
Lightning Source LLC
Chambersburg PA
CBHW021403290426
44108CB00010B/365